GREEK LITERARY CRITICISM

EDITED BY

ERNEST BARKER, M.A., D.LITT., LL.D.

PRINCIPAL OF KING'S COLLEGE, UNIVERSITY OF LONDON

AMS PRESS

NEW YORK

GREEK
LITERARY CRITICISM

BY

J. D. DENNISTON

FELLOW OF HERTFORD COLLEGE,
OXFORD

Shadows we are and
Like shadows depart

1924
LONDON AND TORONTO
J. M. DENT & SONS LTD.
NEW YORK: E. P. DUTTON & CO.

Library of Congress Cataloging in Publication Data

Denniston, John Dewar.
  Greek literary criticism.

    Original ed. issued in series: The Library of Greek
thought.
    Bibliography: p.
    1. Criticism--Greece. I. Title. II. Series:
The Library of Greek thought.
PN87.D4 1973   880'.9   76-163686
ISBN 0-404-07801-X

Reprinted from an original copy in the collections
of the Newark Public Library

Reprinted by arrangement with J.M. Dent & Sons Ltd.
London, England

From the edition of 1924, London
First AMS edition published in 1973
Manufactured in the United States of America

AMS PRESS INC.
NEW YORK, N.Y. 10003

PREFACE

ALMOST all the translations in this book are borrowed, and I am therefore under heavy obligations to the scholars and publishers who have so readily and courteously allowed me to make use of them.

I have to thank Professor Gilbert Murray and Mr. George Allen for the second half of Aristophanes, *Frogs*: the Jowett trustees and the Delegates of the Clarendon Press for passages from Jowett's Plato, *Ion, Gorgias, Phaedrus,* and *Laws*: Professor A. D. Lindsay and Messrs. J. M. Dent and Sons for passages from Plato, *Republic*: the Clarendon Press for passages from the late Professor Bywater's Aristotle, *Poetics*: the Syndics of the Cambridge University Press for passages from the late Sir Richard Jebb's Aristotle, *Rhetoric*: Professor W. Rhys Roberts and Messrs. Macmillan and Co. for passages from Dionysius, *On Literary Composition*: and Professor W. Rhys Roberts and the Syndics of the Cambridge University Press for passages from Dionysius, *The Three Literary Letters,* Longinus, *On the Sublime,* and Demetrius, *On Style.*

The translators' names will be found appended to the various passages, except for the few which I have turned into English myself.

I also have to thank Mr. A. B. Poynton for advice on several passages in Dionysius, and my wife for assistance in proof-reading.

I have tried to make the selections as representative as possible. But the whole side of Greek criticism which deals with the technical minutiae of language had to be

v

omitted because its appreciation depends on a knowledge of Greek. I was for this reason compelled to omit some interesting passages from Dionysius and Demetrius. As far as the book depends on my own labours (luckily not very far) it calls for something more than a formal apology. Like most works of the kind, it has been completed during infrequent intervals of leisure, and amidst many distractions. But I hope, nevertheless, that it may be of some little use in introducing a wider public to an interesting side-walk of the Greek intellect, and directing them to places where they can obtain more information on the subject.

J. D. DENNISTON.

23rd April 1924.

INTRODUCTION

LITERARY criticism is a term not easy to define. In the more limited sense it is the attempt to determine what literature is good and what bad: to discover wherein the goodness or badness consists: and perhaps also to supplement the purely scholastic interpretation of literature by an elucidation of its deeper artistic significance. But it is difficult, or impossible, either to confine the critic wholly within these bounds or to preserve them as his private domain. All around him are neighbours on whom he is at times tempted to encroach, and they on him: the aesthetic philosopher, who tries to discover the essential nature of beauty in the abstract: the moral and political philosophers, who investigate the effect of that beauty on the individual and on the state: the textual scholar, who tries to restore in their integrity the exact words of the works which the critic judges, and in the process must necessarily take into account style as well as manuscript authority: the commentator, whose linguistic and grammatical interpretation of literature cannot be kept entirely separate from its aesthetic exposition: the teacher of literary technique, who, if he is to help people to write well in the future, must learn by what means they wrote well in the past.

In a book like this, it is desirable for many reasons to cover the wider field: first and foremost, because literary criticism of the narrower type occupies quite a subordinate place in Greek literature. It did not often occur to an ancient Greek to say: " I like this work: let us consider why." At any rate, not much was written in Greek with this for an ultimate object.   The main current of Greek literary criticism, if anything so sporadic can be said to have a main current, flowed in the channel of Greek rhetorical theory, a subject which could be treated, according to the taste of the theorist, in a more or a less literary fashion. It might perhaps be expected that rhetorical text-books would not provide very interesting literary criticism, and that they would at any rate tend to ignore the poets.   As a matter of fact this is not so, because the Greeks, although differentiating the vocabularies of prose and poetry more sharply than we do, insisted strongly (and from a modern standpoint excessively) on the unity of all literary expression, whether in prose or in verse.   Thus we find writer after writer on Greek rhetoric not only recommending his pupils to study the poets, not only grouping poets and prose-writers together in the classification of styles, but actually drawing from Homer and the tragedians examples of oratorical devices for the student's imitation.   It happens therefore that the writers on rhetoric, though starting from a different point of departure, contain among their numbers men who must be reckoned either mainly, like Dionysius, or wholly, like Longinus, as literary critics in the modern sense.   And there can be no possibility of excluding them on the ground that their ultimate object in writing was not criticism but practical instruction.   Whether to include aesthetic philo- sophy is at first sight a more difficult question, though in practice almost all writers on Greek literary criticism have included it.   One would perhaps hardly expect to find extracts from Benedetto Croce in an anthology of modern literary criticism.   At the same time aesthetic philosophy must find a place somewhere in a library of Greek thought: and the present place seems on the whole more appropriate than any other.

Criticism for criticism's sake is, as I have indicated, hard to find in Greek literature. We meet it in the essayists of the first and second centuries of the Christian era, Dio Chrysostom, Plutarch and Lucian. In a sense, we meet it much earlier in fifth and fourth century Attic comedy. At least we have one complete and brilliant specimen of it in Aristophanes' *Frogs*, and can dimly descry its presence elsewhere, by the aid of titles and fragments. But its extant bulk is small, its treatment of the subject for the most part desultory and superficial.

It will be seen, then, that under the heading of Greek literary criticism are included writings very different in object, method and character. To attempt a chronological survey of so heterogeneous a mass would only lead to confusion. I propose instead to deal separately with the criticism contained in comedy, the aesthetic theory of the philosophers, and the study of rhetorical technique: and finally to give some account of the criticism which does not come under these heads. No doubt, this method involves certain inconveniences, but I am convinced that it conduces to a clearer view of the evolution of Greek critical theory in its various branches.

Comic poets in fifth-century Athens made fun of everything in the life they saw around them, and it was not to be expected that they should neglect so promising an object of satire as literature. In point of fact, our evidence indicates that literary criticism, of some kind or other, was an important part of the stock-in-trade of the comic stage, from the very earliest performances of comedy at Athens down to the end of the fourth century B.C. It is true that the eleven extant plays of Aristophanes, dating from 425 to 388, are the only complete comedies which have survived from this age. But we possess a considerable collection of fragments and a large number of play titles. The fragments, especially those of certain authors, contain a number of references to literature. The titles are still more significant. For a Greek comedy was usually named after its chorus: and, in general, irrelevant titles seem hardly ever to have been given by authors to their plays. (The *Frogs* is an exception easily explained on particular grounds.[1]) Scanning the list, we meet everywhere such titles as *Poetry*, *The Poet*, *The Muses*, *The Harp-players*, *Sappho* (these last two titles some half-dozen times each), *Tritagonistes* (as the third actor in a play was called), *Herakles the Stage-manager*, *The Rehearsal*, *Phileuripides*, *The Archilochuses* (Archilochus of Paros was the typical severe critic). It is hard to imagine how plays not having literature for their main subject could have been written to such titles.

As to the nature and tendency of the criticism contained in these plays, the evidence is scarcely sufficient to warrant conjecture. Speaking generally, Athenian comedy seems to have had a strong conservative bias, in art as in politics and morals. Many of the fragments from the lost plays suggest well-known passages in Aristophanes. Sometimes the modern poets are ridiculed for their bombastic, pretentious language and their love of sound without sense, sometimes for their metrical experiments. The musical criticism (and it must be remembered that the poets were for the most part musicians also) is a little more definite. The most heinous crimes of the modernists were that they increased the number of lyre-strings, thus making it possible to modulate from one mode to another, and that they made the music more independent of the words, introducing roulades on a single syllable. When, however, we reach the last quarter of the fifth century, the series of Aristophanic comedies throws a flood of light on the state of contemporary criticism. The earliest of the extant comedies, the *Acharnians*, has

[1] The preference for animal titles: perhaps also the fact that the *Frogs* had a chorus of "Mystae": and the title "Mystae" had recently been used by another dramatist.

a delightful scene parodying the sentimental realism of Euripides. The hero, Dicaeopolis, about to plead the enemy's cause at considerable risk to himself, comes to Euripides for the loan of a few rags, to excite the pity of the bench. The whole filthy wardrobe of the tragic heroes (mostly lame or diseased) is ransacked, and Dicaeopolis finally goes off satisfied, after having, as the tragedian pathetically complains, " robbed him of his tragic art."

A later play, the *Thesmophoriazusae*, is more extensively concerned with literary matters. The plot is that the women of Athens, incensed at Euripides' persistent abuse of them, are intending to hatch a plot against him at their festival of Thesmophoria. Euripides, getting wind of this, unsuccessfully tries to persuade his effeminate fellow-poet Agathon to dress up as a woman and conduct his defence at the festival. This gives Aristophanes the opportunity for a scene satirising Agathon, his personal appearance, his poetry and his method of composition. Agathon refuses to lend his services, but Euripides' old cousin Mnesilochus is persuaded to undertake the task of impersonation, is detected by the women and bound to a plank, and after a series of scenes elaborately parodying several of Euripides' more sensational and melodramatic plays, finally escapes.

The whole of the second half of the *Frogs*, in Professor Gilbert Murray's brilliant translation, will be found quoted in this book. The plot of the play is in outline as follows. Euripides and Sophocles are recently dead. The tragic stage is now left deserted, and Dionysus, the patronal deity of the Athenian theatre, descends to the underworld, accompanied by his slave Xanthias, with the object of bringing back Euripides. When he arrives, after sundry adventures, he finds that a contest is about to take place between Euripides and Aeschylus for the possession of the throne of tragedy in Hades. Here our extract begins. Pluto appoints Dionysus judge. The two poets conduct an elaborate attack on each other's works, first of all on ethical and political, subsequently on technical literary grounds. At the end of it all Dionysus does not know which to choose. As a final test, he invites the two to give their respective opinions on the political situation. On the strength of the answers Aeschylus is adjudged victor. But instead of the throne of tragedy, his reward is to return with Dionysus to the upper world, his parting injunction being that Euripides shall never be allowed, by any manner of chance, to occupy the throne.

Aristophanes' plays are valuable for the history of literary criticism, not only on account of the criticism which they contain, but also because of the light they throw on the general state of criticism in his day. In this respect two facts emerge. In the first place, everybody was talking about literature. Strepsiades, the country bumpkin in the *Clouds*, is warned by his instructor Socrates that if he wishes to shine in polite society he must be able to hold his own in a discussion of metrical questions: and smart young men at dinner parties are apt to fire off their views on the relative merits of Aeschylus and Euripides in a pithy sentence or two. In the second place, criticism was becoming more articulate and technical, and was evolving a jargon of its own, not always intelligible to the plain man, and a godsend to the humorist. Euripides in the *Frogs*, and his devoted admirer Dionysus, talk in this style, in sharp contrast to the old-fashioned Aeschylus. Expressions like " Generative poet," " Sinews of tragedy," " Obscure in his statement of the situation," seem to be typical of the new criticism, and to have afforded great delight to the audience; while any reference to a file, a plane or a lathe in connection with Euripides or Agathon (who apparently described the subtleties of composition in terms of the carpenter's shop) was certain to bring down the house. These two poets were undoubtedly much interested in questions of technique. Euripides actually takes the questionable course of introducing literary criticism into his tragedies. In his *Electra* he goes out of his way to pour scorn on the device by which Aeschylus effected the recognition of the hero by the heroine in a play on the same subject. And in his *Phoenissae* he has a hit at the long and undramatic description of the devices on the chieftains' shields in Aeschylus' *Seven against Thebes*. Of Agathon, whose works have perished, we naturally know less. But even among his scanty fragments there are two on the subjects of the relation between art and inspiration and of dramatic probability, which suggest a self-conscious and theoretical-minded artist.

After Aristophanes we have again to fall back upon fragments. But these are plentiful enough to show us that Attic comedy, though it ceased at the end of the fifth century to be political in tone, retained its interest in literature and music. Euripides is still much to the fore: and we now begin to find criticism of prose writers also, among others Demosthenes, who is described as "the devourer of catapults and spears, a fellow who hates literature, and never uttered an antithesis in his life: a man with Ares in his gaze": rather an apt way of hitting off the contrast between Demosthenic intensity and Isocratean polish. Gradually, it is true, criticism disappears from comedy. That is however due, not to waning interest in the subject, but to the supersession of the old topical type of comedy by a new sentimental type on modern romantic lines, with love interest and elaborate plot.

Turning now to the philosophers, we may make Plato our starting-point, for with him Greek aesthetic theory really begins. It is true that long before him Xenophanes and Heraclitus had criticised Homer. But they did so from a purely ethical standpoint. Neither Xenophanes, with his complaint that "Homer and Hesiod attributed to the gods all that is a reproach and scandal among men," nor the ingenious persons who attempted to save Homer's face by allegorising him, really concerned themselves with poetry as such. On the whole, the earlier Greek philosophers were too busy trying to solve the problem of matter, to have any time for other inquiries. And it was not until the Greeks began to study political science that they found themselves confronted with the questions: "What forms of poetry and music should be allowed in the ideal state?" and "What are the true criteria for judging poetry and music?"

Incidental references in Plato's works to artistic topics are numerous and important. But his most systematic treatment of the subject is contained in the *Republic*, of his middle period, and the *Laws*, the work of his old age. His whole attitude to art has been censured for its ethical bias. And it is true that he often seems to assume rather arbitrarily the identification of the beautiful with the good. Two facts, however, must be borne in mind. In the first place, both in the *Republic* and in the *Laws*, Plato is primarily concerned with politics, not with aesthetics. His business is to inquire whether certain forms of art are politically valuable, not whether they may be defended on other grounds. That they may be so defended, he himself occasionally hints: as, for example, in the famous passage. in the *Republic* where he expels the poets from his ideal state, after anointing them with myrrh and crowning them with garlands. But why should they have myrrh and garlands unless, while condemned by a political standard they can be approved by another, and a different, test? In the second place, the Greeks aestheticised their morals so much that they could hardly be expected not to moralise their aesthetics. Using a language in which *kalos* ("beautiful") also meant good, it was impossible for them not to confuse morals and aesthetics to some extent.

The discussion of literature in the *Republic* falls into two parts. The subject is first broached in the third book, where Plato is sketching the education of the guardians of his ideal state: it is resumed, in an altered form, in the tenth and last book. In the third book Plato limits the poet in point of matter and in point of style. The former limitation does not appear to be of great originality or importance. When Plato objects to certain stories in Homer as unedifying, he is only saying what Xenophanes has said long before. (We must remember, in passing, that Homer was to the Greeks of the classical period no mere poet, but a revered, almost sacred, teacher.) The second limitation is a more striking one. The poet is to speak, where possible, *in propria persona*, not through the mouths of his characters. In Plato's words, he must employ "simple narration" rather than *mimesis* (impersonation). Thus not only drama but all speeches in epic are ruled out. The reason for this restriction is that impersonation can find no place in a city where everyone is to look after his own business and leave other people's alone.

When Plato returns to the subject in the tenth book, the treatment is on a different plane. Here we find raised, for the first time in extant Greek literature, fundamental questions in the metaphysic and psychology of art. The discussion starts with an expression of relief that the "mimetic poet" has been banished from the state. But *mimesis* has changed its meaning since we met it in the third book. It now signifies, not impersonation, but the copying of the actual world in art. And as, according to Plato's metaphysics, the actual world is a copy of the ideal, the world as depicted in art must be merely the copy of a copy.

After thus depreciating art on metaphysical grounds, Plato proceeds to attack it on psychological and moral grounds. The easiest and the most popular model for imitation, he says, is the man in whose mind a conflict is raging between a higher and a lower element. The fight against temptation, in fact, is the favourite theme of art. This pre-occupation with the baser part of the soul (so Plato re-states the position, ignoring the consideration that the nobler part is also a combatant, and may prove the victor) has a demoralising effect. Moreover, apart from the question of conflict, poetry feeds and strengthens the emotions and passions, which it should be our object to weaken.

In the *Laws* Plato returns to the task of constructing an ideal state, but one more in accordance with practical possibilities. Again the necessity of laying down an educational system leads him, early in the treatise, to a discussion of art. But this time the argument takes a new turn. Our citizens are to be trained in " good art." But what art is " good " ? That which gives the most pleasure ? But in practice different people take pleasure in different kinds of art. And further, since all art is imitative, surely truth, not pleasure, should be the criterion. It is not enough, however, that the imitation should be true. The object imitated must be beautiful (or " good ": the equivocal *kalos* covers both). And, as men are pleased by imitations of what is akin to them, good men will be pleased by imitations of the good. And so, after all, art can be judged by the pleasure it gives *to the best men.*

It is extremely difficult to estimate as a whole Plato's views upon this subject. It has always been a matter for astonishment that one of the greatest prose stylists who ever lived should have adopted so uncompromisingly hostile an attitude to poetry. To some extent Plato seems to be accepting the verdict of an erroneous metaphysical test.

To some extent also he seems to recoil, with a sort of ascetic fervour, from the madness of poetry which may be so dangerous an enemy to the sanity of philosophy. And yet, in spite of all, he can speak of the educative value of art in the most eloquent and noble language.

Aristotle wrote two treatises on the subject of literature: the *Rhetoric* and the incomplete *Poetics*. His main theory of mimetic art in general, and poetry in particular, is to be found in the latter work. Although Plato is not mentioned by name, Aristotle is clearly much pre-occupied with the task of answering him. Thus, for example, Plato's contention that poetry, being a form of imitation, must be judged by the standard of truth, not of pleasure, is met by the reply that correct imitation is in itself a source of pleasure. Against Plato's postulate that the object imitated must be beautiful, it is urged that imitations of ugly things can be beautiful. Plato had objected to poetry because it excites the emotions. "So it does," answers Aristotle, "but by exciting them it releases them, and so its ultimate effect is to make men less emotional." Plato had condemned poetry as an imitation of an imitation. "But," Aristotle replies, "there is a certain philosophic universality in the poetic treatment of a subject, which differentiates poetry from history." Lastly, in the *Politics*, Aristotle meets the Platonic contention that few people are wise, and therefore competent to judge art, by the ingenious, if unconvincing, argument that, though no member of a crowd knows much individually, collectively they know a great deal, each supplying his neighbour's deficiency: their common verdict is therefore correct.

Although, both in the *Poetics* and in the *Rhetoric*, Aristotle is at great pains to give a philosophical rationale of the art with which he is dealing, neither work is wholly, or perhaps even primarily, a philosophical treatise. (One of

B

Aristotle's most remarkable characteristics, in fact, is his power of combining abstract speculation with a keen vision of the practical.) And it will perhaps be convenient to interrupt for a moment our sketch of the history of Greek aesthetic, in order to give some account of the two works. The *Poetics*, according to an ancient Greek authority, consisted originally of two books. The second was lost, probably at a very early period: we possess now what appears to be a fairly complete copy of the first book. It seems highly probable, for various reasons, that the lost second book contained an account of comedy and also of the doctrine of "purgation." The work as we have it opens with an account of the various "imitative" arts, including poetry. Aristotle then goes on to account for the innate naturalness of the love of poetry, and to sketch the early history of the art and the evolution of its various types. Coming to tragedy, he gives in the sixth chapter his famous definition of it. He then divides tragedy into what he calls its "formative elements": Plot, Characters, Diction, Thought, Spectacle, and Melody. The major part of the remainder of the treatise is spent in an examination of these six elements, the greatest importance being attributed to plot. The work ends with a comparison between tragic and epic poetry.

The *Rhetoric*, which, according to an ancient tradition, Aristotle wrote as an improvement on Isocrates' unphilosophical treatment of the subject, is in three books. In the first, after defining the function of rhetoric and distinguishing between the various kinds of proof, Aristotle describes the three types of rhetoric, deliberative, forensic and epideictic (the kind of oratory used on ceremonial occasions). In the second he begins with an elaborate analysis of the emotions, it being one of the orator's objects to arouse emotion in his hearers, and goes on to give examples of certain universal methods of argument which can be applied *mutatis mutandis* to any case. In the third book, which is the one of most importance from the point of view of literary criticism, Aristotle deals with diction, prose rhythm, the structure of sentences and the arrangement of the different parts of a speech.

The history of Greek aesthetic theory after Aristotle may be indicated in a few sentences. The Peripatetic school, which Aristotle founded, showed a lively interest in literary matters, if we may judge from the titles of numerous lost works. But neither they nor the Stoics, who occupied themselves particularly with grammar, seem to have advanced the theory of art in any material way. Perhaps the most interesting aesthetic observation which has come down to us from the three centuries after Aristotle is the assertion of a certain Philodemus of Gadara, an Epicurean who lived in the closing years of the first century B.C., that music, of itself, has no power whatever to "imitate" character, or even (a surprising statement) to arouse, intensify or allay emotion. It would be interesting to follow the arguments on which Philodemus bases this violent reaction against the "imitation" theory. But the papyrus discovered at Herculaneum which is our sole authority for the text of his *De Musica*, though intact enough to stimulate curiosity, is too mutilated to satisfy it.

While Philodemus attacks the mimetic view of art for claiming too much, the tendency of aesthetic theory in the early centuries of the Christian era is to attack it for claiming too little. The inadequacy of the view was indicated, even before Plato's exposition of it, by Socrates, who laid stress, if we may believe Xenophon's account, on the artist's power to select and combine objects for imitation, and so, in a sense, to create a new thing. And when Aristotle, in order to meet the facts, is constrained to admit that a poet may "imitate" either what exists or what might exist, he is putting a severe strain on the elasticity of the word "imitate." When again he observes that poetry is "more universal" than history, he seems to be on the verge of a radical modification of the imitation theory. But the modification is not made, and we have to wait till the first century A.D. for a re-statement of the artist's *modus operandi*. Dio Chrysostom (50–117 A.D.), an itinerant lecturer from Bithynia, in his oration ("lecture" would be a more appropriate rendering) "On knowing God," remarks that "painters and sculptors invest the God with the human body, the vessel of wisdom and reason, seeking to manifest the imageless and unseen in the visible, which can be portrayed." (The translation is the late Professor Bernard Bosanquet's.) In the same manner Philostratus, in the early third century, speaking of Pheidias' sculptures of the Gods, says: "It was imagination that wrought these forms, a more cunning artist than imitation. Imitation will make what it has seen, but imagination will make what it has not seen." (Bosanquet's translation.) Earlier Greek had no word for "imagination." Philostratus uses "phantasia," which to Aristotle had meant nothing more than "feeble perception," the half-faded recollection of something once experienced. The need felt for a word meaning "imagination" is symptomatic of a considerable advance in aesthetic theory. Finally, the neo-Platonist Plotinus (205–270 A.D.) defends art against Plato's attack in terms of Plato's own metaphysics, when he says boldly: "We must bear in mind that the arts do not simply imitate the visible, but go back to the reasons from which nature comes; and further that they create much out of themselves, and add to that which is defective, as being themselves in possession of beauty." (Bosanquet's translation.) This improved view of the metaphysical basis of art is the last achievement of Greek aesthetic philosophy. It is now time to turn to the rhetoricians.

The Greeks themselves attributed the rise of their rhetoric to the Sicilian revolution, which expelled the tyrants from Agrigentum and Syracuse in 472 and 466 B.C. The consequent upheaval of social order and the frequency of claims for restitution of property increased litigation and gave an impetus to the study of oratory as an art. A certain Corax and his pupil Tisias, who flourished in Sicily at this time, are reputed to have been the first professors of rhetoric. It appears, however, that they confined themselves to the discussion of subject matter, the presentation and arrangement of arguments. The pioneer in the evolution of Greek prose style, a man who exercised a lasting influence on Greek literature, was another Sicilian, a certain Gorgias of Leontini. Gorgias came on an embassy to Athens in 427, and produced an immediate and profound effect on a nation trained in the appreciation of poetry, but as yet ignorant of the possibilities of artistic prose. His style had two principal features. It was poetical in vocabulary, and consisted of symmetrical and elaborately balanced, often rhyming, clauses. (It is curious to find rhyme, which classical Greek poetry never adopted, appearing thus early in prose.) A few fragments of Gorgias survive. They read rather like an exaggerated parody of his pupil Isocrates. Actually it was Isocrates who modified the exaggerations of Gorgias. It is easy to laugh at Gorgias now. But his contribution to the history of literature is no slight one. In reality, he and others supplied the technique into which later writers infused the intellectual and emotional content, in much the same way as the musical composers of the sixteenth century poured their emotion into a technical mould inherited from their predecessors.

Of almost equal importance is the Chalcedonian Thrasy-

machus, who was already resident in Athens when Gorgias
arrived there.   Thrasymachus is most widely known from
Plato's attack, in the *Republic*, on his radical opinions.
But there can be little doubt that he contributed largely
to the moulding of Greek style.   He was interested in
prose rhythm, and recommended the use of a foot called the
first paeon (a long syllable followed by three shorts) for the
beginning of a sentence, and the last paeon (three shorts
followed by a long) for the end of it.   His extant fragments,
however, show no trace of obedience to his own precept.
What they do show is a marked faculty for the construction
of organised, periodic sentences, which stand far nearer to
the rich, easy flow of fourth-century prose than to the
choppy aridity of Gorgias.   While it is possible to form a
fairly definite idea of the styles of Gorgias and Thrasymachus,
it is less easy to estimate their capacity as teachers and
theorists, with which we are here more especially concerned.   Thrasymachus certainly wrote an *Art of Rhetoric*.
Whether Gorgias also wrote one, is not certain.   It seems
probable that both men preferred example to precept, and
that, although they laid down certain general rules for
observance, they relied mainly on giving samples of every
conceivable kind of speech for their pupils' imitation.   This
lack of systematic theory was undoubtedly the weak point
of the early teachers of rhetoric.   Their method, as Aristotle says, was "rapid, but unscientific: professing to
bestow an art, they in fact only bestowed its products: as
though one were to promise a man to tell him the secret
of always having comfortable feet, and then present him
with a number of pairs of shoes."

Gorgias' pupil Isocrates, who started life as a lawyer,
but quickly abandoned this career for that of a political
pamphleteer, wrote an *Art of Rhetoric*.   Quite a number
of people must have written " Arts " in the fourth century,

for Aristotle, who was a pupil of Isocrates, thought it worth while to collect them into a kind of corpus. With Aristotle's own contribution to the subject I have dealt above. Another extant work on rhetoric of this period is the so-called *Rhetorica ad Alexandrum*, attributed to Aristotle, but now thought to be by Anaximenes, a rhetorician who accompanied Alexander on his eastern campaigns. It only touches incidentally on questions of style, and, though interesting as a specimen of the rhetorical handbooks of the day, and as contrasted with Aristotle's more philosophical treatment of the subject, merits no more than a passing reference here.

Aristotle's successor as head of the Peripatetic school, Theophrastus (372–287 B.C.), wrote a number of rhetorical treatises, which must have enjoyed a long popularity, as Dionysius, three centuries later, constantly refers to them. Little is known of Theophrastus' views on rhetoric, but he certainly discussed, and is by some thought to have originated, the classification of styles into certain characteristic types, a topic which figures largely in later writers.

With the death of Theophrastus we come to a wide gap in the history of Greek rhetorical theory. It appears, indeed, that for fully a century and a half there existed no theory worth mentioning. These were bad days for Rhetoric, and her old enemy Philosophy was in the ascendant. Such oratory as there was, flourished on the mainland of Asia Minor and the islands off that coast. But the Asiatic style, as it was afterwards called, had little enough merit, if we may judge by the few fragments of it which have survived, and by the uniformly unfavourable verdict of the ancient critics. Its main exponent, the *bête noir* of the purists of a later age, was a certain Hegesias of Magnesia. His extant fragments are chiefly characterised by

what Jebb well describes as a " curious combination of jerki-
ness and magniloquence." This was the style which
reigned supreme during the later third century B.C. and
the greater part of the second. And when the Romans
began (about 130 B.C.) to study prose-writing seriously,
this was the style which they took as their model. But
already there were signs of a coming reaction. Hermagoras
of Temnos (who flourished probably about 150-25 B.C.)
revived rhetorical theory. And though he confined himself
to the academic discussion of subject matter, the Rhodian
professors of the following generation initiated the systematic
stylistic study of the great Athenian orators. During the
course of the first century B.C. this " Atticising " reaction
accumulated force. Its Rhodian originators were left
behind in the race, and were later regarded as occupying an intermediate position between the extreme Asiatics
and the extreme Atticists. Cicero himself was Rhodian
trained, having studied under a professor named Molon in
the island. Rome was now the main battle-ground of the
contending factions. By about 60 B.C., when Cicero was
in his forties, the Attic reaction had reached its height.
Among its stoutest champions were Caecilius of Kale Akte
in Sicily, and Dionysius, a native of Halicarnassus, the
birthplace of Herodotus. The works of Caecilius, of which
only insignificant fragments remain, were almost all concerned with literature. He wrote *On the Difference between
the Attic and Asiatic Styles, Against the Phrygians* (an uncomplimentary sobriquet for the Asiatics), comparisons between
Aeschines and Demosthenes and Demosthenes and Cicero,
essays on Lysias, a book on the Ten Orators (the ten
Orators of the so-called Attic Canon, which was,
perhaps, invented by Caecilius himself) and a treatise *On
the Sublime.*

Dionysius of Halicarnassus, the friend and slightly

younger contemporary of Caecilius, was resident in Rome at least during the years 30–8 B.C., and perhaps later. His most extensive work, and probably the one on which he would have wished his reputation to rest, is the *Roman Antiquities*. But it is mainly as a professor of rhetoric and a literary critic that he is remembered to-day. In mere bulk of extant work he is the most important of all the Greek literary critics. And, without real genius perhaps, he possessed industry, method and talents of no mean order. We possess from his pen a treatise *On the Arrangement of Words* (covering such topics as structure of sentences, word order, euphony and rhythm, and complementary to another treatise, which he projected, but apparently never wrote, on the *Choice of Words*); fragments of a work on *Imitation* (how to imitate classical models); essays on Attic orators, prefaced by a sketch of the decline and revival of oratory (the Asiatic and Atticist movements, that is) and by an exhortation to all aspiring speakers to study the great masters of the past; an essay on Thucydides, and three others, in the form of letters, on various literary subjects. An *Art of Rhetoric* ascribed to him is now generally held to be by another, and a later, hand.

Dionysius' reputation would perhaps have stood higher if less of his work had survived. After reading almost any one of his essays, one is struck with the business-like competence with which he hits off the strong and weak points of his various authors: a competence lit up here and there by flashes of real insight, like his criticism of Thucydides' "old world and masterful nobility of style," or Plato's "mellow and imperceptible tinge of antiquity." But after reading two or three essays, the sameness of the method becomes apparent. Dionysius always seems to be fitting his criticisms into a ready-made framework. He is somewhat at the mercy of his own words, as he accuses Isocrates of

being. He is too like a judge at a competitive musical
festival, allotting so many marks for intonation, so many
for tone, so many for ensemble, etc. He has not very much
real enthusiasm for literature. His criticism of Demosthenes
is one of the few passages in which he is really carried away.
Not that perpetual " Schwärmerei " is a mark of good
criticism. But, as the work of the greatest critics shows,
enthusiasm may be communicated without being directly
expressed. And the passages which Dionysius selects for
commendation do not, on the whole, show that sense for
literature which Longinus, for example, possesses. Moreover, if at times Dionysius rises above the level of sound
common sense, at times he falls far below it. He is, without
any doubt, right in maintaining that Thucydides sometimes
sacrifices lucidity to terseness. But the attempt to re-write
so subtly pregnant an author as Thucydides is precarious,
and Dionysius fails in it lamentably. Plato, or Plato at
least in the noblest of his moods, he simply cannot understand. He brushes aside, without discussion, the very idea
of the admissibility of poetical prose. He pronounces
Plato inferior to Demosthenes on the score of the funeral
speech in the *Menexenus*. But the speech is quite possibly a parody of Pericles' funeral oration in Thucydides:
and, if it is not a parody, the gross unfairness of representing Plato by such a work should have been obvious.
It is sometimes said that Dionysius' minute disquisitions
on the emotional effect of certain rhythms and certain
letters of the alphabet are a useful antidote to the vagueness
of much modern criticism. And so they might be if they
were scientific. But what can be more unscientific, more
puerile even, than the passage in which he essays to prove
that the rhythm of prose approximates to that of verse by
quoting a passage from Thucydides, hunting out as many
examples as he can of his favourite feet, manufacturing a

few more by the aid of mis-scansion, and then exclaiming triumphantly, " Can all this be coincidence ? " ?

The treatise *On the Sublime* is inscribed with the name of Longinus, minister to Zenobia, queen of Palmyra in the third century A.D. But modern scholars agree that it is a much earlier work, not later probably than the first century of our era. For the sake of brevity, however, it will be convenient to refer to the unknown author as Longinus. The English title, established by long usage, is a singularly misleading one. " On Genius " would scarcely perhaps be too wide. Like Dionysius, Longinus was an Atticist, and exalted " imitation " in a way scarcely intelligible to our own age, which sets originality before everything. We should scarcely agree, for instance, that one author could supply inspiration to another: still less that if a man wishes to write well he should perpetually be saying to himself, " How would Plato or Demosthenes have expressed this ? " But Longinus is far less hide-bound than Dionysius: indeed he is remarkably free from dogmatism and pedantry. Take for example his treatment of metaphor. " Not more than two at a time, and when in doubt put in an ' as it were ' or ' sort of,' " is the Aristotelian precept, dutifully echoed in Demetrius' *On Style*. Longinus goes deeper. " First stir your hearer," he says in essence, "and he will not stop to count your metaphors: and the metaphors will help to stir him yet more. Thus passion helps metaphor and metaphor passion. And the same is true in general of all the devices of language." Surely the relation between expression and technique has never been put more simply and more profoundly. *Mutatis mutandis* a musician might well say the same of inversion and augmentation and other devices of the fugue. This freedom from formalism, which makes even the treatment of " figures " throb with life, is no doubt mainly to be attributed to Longinus' native genius and intense admiration for great writing. But his literary antecedents may also have helped him here. It has been suggested, with some reason, that he was influenced by Theodorus of Gadara, a rhetorical professor of the Augustan age. Now Theodorus did not believe in fixed rules for writing. Here he differed from his contemporary Apollodorus of Pergamum, who did believe in them, and who regarded rhetoric as a science, not an art. Apollodorus is known to have influenced Dionysius. And Longinus seems to be writing in conscious opposition to Dionysius and Caecilius. It was his dissatisfaction with Caecilius' treatment of the "sublime," he tells us, that moved him to write on the subject himself; while the pith and kernel of his work (that "the divine fire," as Beethoven called it, is what really matters in literature, not mere freedom from faults) constitutes a complete negation of Dionysius' rather peddling tabulation of merits and defects.

In general, it can hardly be denied that Longinus is a critic of quite outstanding genius, and it is a matter for congratulation that, after being neglected throughout the nineteenth century, he is coming back into something of the esteem which he possessed in the seventeenth and eighteenth. His work is one which gains in value on each successive reading. Time after time, a sure instinct leads him to the heart of a matter, where others had but scratched the surface. Take his definition of a classic: his psychological analysis of the pleasure derived from great literature: or his account of the relation between emotion and technique, to which reference has been made above. In every case Longinus has something both original and fundamental to say: and says it, too, in the best possible way. For his style, which combines much that is Platonic with a peculiar burning intensity that is all Longinus' own, is no unworthy vehicle of his thought.

From Longinus to *Demetrius on Style* is a steep descent. This book is ascribed to Demetrius of Phalerum, the last of the fourth-century Attic orators. But it is patently of a much later date: and the most probable supposition is that the author was some other Demetrius (the name is a very common one), possibly of the first century A.D. It begins with an analysis of sentence-building, in which the author treats of the number and length of " members " (*cola*) and their combination in periods. But the greater part of the work is a description of the four types of style, the " elevated," the " elegant," the " plain " and the " forcible," and the four corresponding perversions, the " frigid," the " affected," the " arid," and the " graceless." Each type is considered in all its aspects, subject-matter, diction and metaphor, arrangement of words, figures of speech, etc. The writer follows the Peripatetic school, constantly and respectfully quoting Aristotle and Theophrastus. His treatise reads like the work of a diligent compiler, with little distinction of mind or individuality of style. It lacks alike the living inspiration of Longinus and the rather pompous self-importance of Dionysius.

By the end of the second century A.D. the literary impulse which the Atticist revival gave to oratorical theory had died down. In Hermogenes of Tarsus, who flourished about 170 A.D., and to an even greater degree in his successors, the mechanical formulation of rules has replaced the vital appreciation of classical models. The study of rhetoric has crystallised into formality, and here parts company with the study of literature.

After traversing the main highways of our subject, it remains to scour the by-paths, and finally to attempt some estimate of the tendencies and the value of Greek literary criticism as a whole.

As to the former task, even a summary review cannot

wholly neglect the scholars who, during the third, second and first centuries B.C., at Alexandria and Pergamum, and latterly at Rome, devoted laborious lives to the collecting, cataloguing, emending and interpreting of the great authors of the creative period which had ended.   A brief mention will suffice.   The works of these scholars, Zenodotus, Aristophanes of Byzantium, Aristarchus, and other lesser names, have perished, but much of their doctrine survives.   For while little original work was done in scholarship between the Christian era and the Renaissance, the labours of the Alexandrian critics were collected and peptonised by such men as Didymus, in the reign of Augustus, were handed down from generation to generation, and finally reach us in the margins of the mediaeval manuscripts which have · preserved for us the classical texts themselves.   It was observed at the beginning of this essay that interpretation and criticism are nearly allied.   And in fact no one can go very far in the first without to some extent touching the second.   Scholars like Verrall and Wilamowitz are also literary critics in the fullest sense of the term.   But the Alexandrian scholars never made the transition, for the reason that they did not go deep enough into interpretation. They were mainly and essentially concerned with the letter, not with the spirit.   When Aristarchus remarked that we must read Homer in the light of Homer, not in the light of our own age, he was asserting a principle fundamental to literary criticism as well as to scholarship, and one too often forgotten even by ourselves, who boast of our historical spirit.   But the Alexandrians did not often light upon such truths, and indeed were not primarily concerned to look for them.   More important for our purpose are the writers of *belles lettres*, who from the first century of our era onwards turned out in profusion more or less popular essays on all imaginable subjects, literature among them:

men like Plutarch, Dio Chrysostom and Lucian, who, dissimilar as they are in most respects, may suitably be grouped together for our purpose, in view of the occasional and unsystematic character of their writings on literature.

Plutarch (50-100 A.D.) provides several promising titles, but the contents are disappointing.   What interested him was not so much literature as morals and education (as in *How a Young Man should listen to Poetry*) or politics (as in *The Malignity of Herodotus*, if indeed Plutarch wrote it). His *Comparison of Aristophanes and Menander* is superficial criticism, but I give an extract from it, as we have a number of similar titles of lost works by other authors, and it is of interest to see what at least one of them was like.   My other extract from Plutarch expresses an important truth too often forgotten, that the listener or reader, as well as the author, has a task to perform: true listening is not merely sitting passive and having words poured into you.

Dio has already been mentioned for the advance which he made in the metaphysic of aesthetic.   We see him as a critic pure and simple in the *Philoctetes*, where he discusses the different ways in which Aeschylus, Sophocles and Euripides handled the same story.   Dio's treatment of the theme is not very illuminating, or profound, though the piece is pleasantly enough written.   It seems curious that other Greek critics should not have attempted this comparative method, when one thinks of the numerous cases in which the same plot was used by different dramatists.

Lucian, a Syrian of Samosata on the Euphrates, who lived from about 120 to 200 A.D., is a much more entertaining person.   Apprenticed in boyhood to a sculptor, he ran away and trained himself as an advocate, practising for a time at Antioch.   Subsequently he toured Greece, Italy and Gaul as a professional lecturer.   Later he retired from this occupation, and spent the remainder of his life in his native land. As a brilliant stylist in a language not originally his own, Lucian may be compared with Mr. Belloc, whom indeed he resembles in some other respects. He has some of the qualities of both Aristophanes and Plato, more subtly ironic than the first, more robust than the second. Charlatanry, affectation and pompousness were the qualities he most hated, and he attacked them wherever he found them, or thought he found them, in literature as in life. He particularly disliked the sham archaism and classicism of the day. The passage I quote from *The Orator's Manual* illustrates his views on this subject: so does the *Lexiphanes*, a dialogue in which one of the speakers talks in language so unintelligible that he has to be purged of archaisms by the administering of a powerful emetic. In *How to write History* Lucian censures the use of poetical language in historical composition: otherwise he concerns himself more with the matter than with the manner of history.

In reviewing the whole course of Greek literary criticism and attempting to measure its achievements, perhaps the first thing that strikes one is the predominant position occupied by the prose-writers, particularly the orators. On the subject of poetry we possess one play by Aristophanes and one technical treatise by Aristotle. As against this, we have numerous detailed judgments of the principal Greek prose-writers, and several elaborate expositions of the whole apparatus of prose expression. The reason for this disparity is that the bulk of the criticism we possess originates in the effort to purify oratorical style by bringing it back to Attic principles. How far should we find the same disparity if we had all the Greek criticism that was ever written, instead of a quantitatively trifling proportion? This question, which we cannot help asking, is not easy to answer. We certainly possess the titles, from early in the fourth century B.C., of a very large number of works dealing not only with such general subjects as "The Beautiful," "Poetry," and "Music," but with particular poets, Homer (par excellence), Hesiod, Epicharmus (the early Sicilian comedian), Thespis (the founder of Attic tragedy), Euripides, "The Tragic Authors," and so on. But we have no means whatever of gauging the merit, or conjecturing the scope, of these works. It is true that considerable fragments have recently been discovered of a *Life of Euripides* by a certain Satyrus, a writer of the third century B.C. They are an uncritical farrago of biographical details, with a few attempts at criticism of a superficial kind and an abundance of anecdotic scandal. It is impossible to tell whether Satyrus' work is typical of its class. If so, we can form no high opinion of this genre, though we must, no doubt, regret the loss of much valuable information.

In the second place, Greek criticism is intensely conservative. Whatever the popular view may have been, the critics all look back rather than forward. Timotheus' words, " I sing not the old songs, for the new are far better," find no echo in Greek criticism. This perpetual *laudatio temporis acti* is a depressing feature in instructional works. Dionysius can have had no hope whatever that any of his readers would approach the performances of the great classical orators. He knew, for he tells us so in discussing Dinarchus, that mere imitation leads only to the production of second-hand, second-rate work, which a good judge can easily distinguish from the original. Yet he exhorted his readers to make imitation their sheet-anchor, because, apparently, he was convinced that a second-hand copy of Demosthenes was better than anything they would be likely to produce out of their own heads. Perhaps after all he was right. Wilamowitz says that Dionysius and his brother Atticists destroyed the creative power in Greek literature. But it is arguable that the creative power was already dead,

c

and that the Attic reaction was merely a necessary acknowledgment of literary bankruptcy.

It was not, however, only in the first century B.C. that
Greek criticism was unprogressive.   It had been equally so
in the great productive centuries, the fifth and the fourth.
The comic poets and Plato are invariably on the side of the
ancients and against the moderns.   In the case of the comic
poets, this may be partly because it is more amusing to
attack one's contemporaries than one's ancestors.   But both
the comic poets and Plato had other reasons for their artistic
conservatism.   Literature was far more closely connected
then than now with politics and morals.   And it is possible
that Aristophanes would have given a much more favourable
verdict on Euripides if he had not seen in him the literary
representative of social and political tendencies which he
detested.   There is evidence that he found much to admire
in Euripides the poet, had he been able to forget Euripides
the iconoclast.   In fact, his rivals on the comic stage accused
him of imitating Euripides' style, and he half admitted the
impeachment himself.   As to Plato, his ethical bias has
already been discussed.   Nowhere perhaps is it more strongly
expressed than in a passage in the *Laws*, where he tells us
that the Egyptians ensured the permanence of their constitution by forbidding innovations in music.   " Let me make a
nation's songs, and I care not who make its laws."

Thirdly, Greek critics suffer from a certain formalism,
a delight in technical terminology and elaborate classification
for their own sake.   (Even Longinus is not quite free from
this tendency, which makes Aristotle at times such weary
reading.)   They credit theory with the power to explain
and perform everything, and are reluctant to leave anything
in literature unaccounted for.   They exalt technique and
training at the expense of genius, individuality and inspiration.
Plato, it is true, attributes much to inspiration, but he

writes as though opposing received opinion: and besides, there is more than a touch of malice in Plato's insistence on the inspired origin of literature, and his consequent denial of its rationality.

Fourthly, with all their belief in the power of analysis, and their almost fanatical veneration for the classics, the Greek literary critics were curiously reluctant to submit the classics to systematic analysis. They were far too apt to adopt views either a priori or on an insufficient examination of the evidence. It has often been remarked, for instance, that Aristotle fixes his attention almost exclusively upon a single play, the *Oedipus Tyrannus* of Sophocles. It is sometimes simply impossible to square his theories with the practice of the Greek tragedians as a whole. Or take the subject of prose rhythm. Here is a question which interested most of the Greek critics from Thrasymachus in the fifth century B.C. to Demetrius in the first A.D. Yet during all this period no advance whatever was made, simply because no one was prepared to take the trouble to compile statistical evidence. Our own generation has taken the trouble to compile such statistics, and as a consequence, though we are still at the beginning of the subject, tangible and important results have been reached at once. Much the same may be said of Dionysius' analysis of the emotional effect of different letters of the alphabet. A scientific inquiry on these lines, which covered a wide ground, might yield valuable fruit. But Dionysius' method is totally un-scientific, his field absurdly restricted.

Fifthly, it is singular to observe how completely the later Greek critics ignored Latin literature. When Dionysius wrote, Vergil and Horace were at their height, Lucretius, Catullus and Cicero had lived. Yet the opportunity for comparing two great literatures was, with a single exception, completely neglected. The comparison of

Demosthenes and Cicero seems to have been a favourite topic. Apart from Cicero, not one Roman author is so much as named by the Greek critics, even by Dionysius, who lived in Rome for many years and was a diligent student of Roman history.

And yet, in spite of the limitations, whether inevitable or self-imposed, of their outlook, and in spite of a certain under-estimation of the difficulties of their task which sometimes led them to make sweeping statements without adequate examination of the ground, the importance of the Greek critics is very considerable. They enunciated with great clearness, if with an excess of rigour, most of the principles fundamental to literary excellence. They indicated, though they did not always follow up, the main lines of advance in criticism. At their best, they are masters of their craft: at their worst, they are at any rate enterprising and interesting pioneers.

BIBLIOGRAPHY

In appreciating criticism, it is helpful to have some knowledge of the object criticised. Many of those who read this book will probably be acquainted, at least through translations, with Homer and the tragedians. But the Greek prose-writers, and in particular the orators, who occupied the attention of the Greek critics so largely, are less widely known. Now, however, thanks to the Loeb library, translations of even the lesser Attic orators are appearing, and it is possible to obtain accurate and readable versions of almost all the writers criticised.

For getting some idea of the general development of Greek literature, Professor Gilbert Murray's delightful *Ancient Greek Literature* may be used: or, if quite a short sketch is required, the section on Greek literature in the *Cambridge Companion to Greek Studies*.

For translations of the Greek literary critics themselves, I may, to avoid needless repetition, refer to the preface. I will add that Bywater's *Poetics* and Rhys Roberts' Dionysius (*On Literary Composition* and *The Three Literary Letters*) are all works on a big scale with introduction, text, translation and notes: but that Bywater's translation of the *Poetics* is also published separately in a cheap edition. Professor Rhys Roberts' monumental works are of the greatest possible value to all students of the subject: and I may perhaps be allowed to pay my tribute of admiration to the masterly skill with which he has reproduced the peculiar qualities of Longinus' style. It is much to be hoped that he will before long give us a translation of the remaining rhetorical writings of Dionysius.

Of modern books on Greek literary criticism the most important are Emile Egger's *Essai sur l'Histoire de la Critique chez les Grecs* (2nd edition, Paris, 1885) and the first part of the first volume of Professor Saintsbury's *History of Criticism*. W. P. Johnston's *Greek Literary Criticism*, the Chancellor's Essay for 1907 (Oxford, B. H. Blackwell), is full of interesting points. The first 119 pages of the late Professor Bernard Bosanquet's *History of Aesthetic* are invaluable for the study of the philosophical side of Greek criticism. For its rhetorical side the reader may consult Jebb's *Attic Orators*, especially the first chapter of the first volume and the last of the second.

CONTENTS

VIII. PLUTARCH

IX. DIO CHRYSOSTOM

X. LUCIAN

GREEK LITERARY CRITICISM

I. ARISTOPHANES

A Contest for the Throne of Tragedy

FROGS 756–1533. (Dionysus' slave Xanthias is conversing with
Aeacus, the porter of Hades.)

Xanthias. What is that noise . . . those shouts and quarrel-
ling. . . . Inside ?
Aeacus. That ? Aeschylus and Euripides!
Xanthias. Eh ?
Aeacus. Yes; there's a big business just astir,
And hot dissension among all the dead.
Xanthias. About what ?
Aeacus. There's a law established here
Concerning all the large and liberal arts,
Which grants the foremost master in each art
Free entertainment at the Central Hearth,
And also a special throne in Pluto's row . . .
Xanthias. Oh, now I understand!
Aeacus. To hold until
There comes one greater; then he must make way.
Xanthias. But how has this affected Aeschylus ?
Aeacus. Aeschylus held the throne of tragedy,
As greatest . . .
Xanthias. Held it ? Why, who holds it now ?
Aeacus. Well, when Euripides came down, he gave
Free exhibitions to our choicest thieves,

I

Footpads, cut-purses, burglars, father-beaters,
—Of whom we have numbers here ; and when they
    heard
The neat retorts, the fencing, and the twists,
They all went mad and thought him something splendid.
And he, growing proud, laid hands upon the throne
Where Aeschylus sat.

Xanthias.   And wasn't pelted off ?

Aeacus. Not he. The whole folk clamoured for a trial
  To see which most was master of his craft.

Xanthias. The whole jail-folk ?

Aeacus.   Exactly;—loud as trumpets.

Xanthias. And were there none to fight for Aeschylus ?

Aeacus. Goodness is scarce, you know. [*Indicating the
    audience*] The same as here!

Xanthias. And what does Pluto mean to do about it ?

Aeacus. Why, hold a trial and contest on the spot
  To test their skill for certain

Xanthias [*reflecting*].   But, I say,
  Sophocles surely must have claimed the throne ?

Aeacus. Not he; as soon as ever he came down,
  He kissed old Aeschylus, and wrung his hand,
  And Aeschylus made room on half his seat.
  And now he means to wait—or so, at least,
  Clidemides informs us—in reserve.
  If Aeschylus wins the day, he'll rest content:
  If not, why then, he says, for poor Art's sake,
  He must show fight against Euripides!

Xanthias. It is to be, then ?

Aeacus.   Certainly, quite soon.
  Just where you stand we'll have the shock of war.
  They'll weigh the poetry line by line . . .

Xanthias.   Poor thing,
  A lamb set in the meat-scale and found wanting!

Aeacus. They'll bring straight-edges out, and cubit-rules,
  And folded cube-frames . . .
Xanthias.   Is it bricks they want ?
Aeacus. And mitre-squares and wedges!   Line by line
  Euripides will test all tragedies!
Xanthias. That must make Aeschylus angry, I should
        think ?
Aeacus. Well, he did stoop and glower like a mad bull.
Xanthias. Who'll be the judge ?
Aeacus.   That was a difficulty.
  Both found an utter dearth of proper critics;
  For Aeschylus objected to the Athenians . . .
Xanthias. Perhaps he thought the jail-folk rather many ?
Aeacus. And all the world beside, he thought mere dirt
  At seeing what kind of thing a poet was.
  So, in the end, they fixed upon your master
  As having much experience in the business.
  But come in; when the master's face looks grave
  There's mostly trouble coming for the slave.
                    [*They go into the house.*
Chorus. [*The song is a parody of the metre and style of
    Aeschylus.*] Eftsoons shall dire anger interne be the
        Thunderer's portion,
    When his foe's glib tusk fresh whetted for blood he
        descries;
    Then fell shall his heart be, and mad; and a pallid
        distortion
      Descend as a cloud on his eyes.
  Yea, words with plumes wild on the wind and with
        helmets a-glancing,
    With axles a-splinter and marble a-shiver, eftsoons
  Shall bleed, as a man meets the shock of a Thought-
        builder's prancing
      Stanzas of dusky dragoons.

The deep crest of his mane shall uprise as he slowly
   unlimbers
   The long-drawn wrath of his brow, and lets loose
      with a roar
Epithets welded and screwed, like new torrent-swept
   timbers
      Blown loose by a giant at war.
Then rises the man of the Mouth; then battleward
   flashes
   A tester of verses, a smooth and serpentine tongue,
To dissect each phrase into mincemeat, and argue to ashes
   That high-towered labour of lung!

*The door opens again. Enter Euripides, Dionysus,
and Aeschylus.*

Euripides. Pray, no advice to me!   I won't give way; I
   claim that I'm more master of my art.
Dionysus. You hear him, Aeschylus. Why don't you
   speak ?
Euripides. He wants to open with an awful silence—
   The blood-curdling reserve of his first scenes.
Dionysus. My dear sir, I must beg! Control your
   language.
Euripides. I know him; I've seen through him years ago;
   Bard of the "noble savage," wooden-mouthed,
   No door, no bolt, no bridle to his tongue,
   A torrent of pure bombast—tied in bundles!
Aeschylus [*breaking out*]. How say'st thou, Son o' the
   goddess of the Greens ?—
   You dare speak thus of me, you phrase-collector,
   Blind-beggar-bard and scum of rifled rag-bags!
   Oh, you shall rue it!
Dionysus.   Stop! Stop, Aeschylus;
   Strike not thine heart to fire on rancour old.

Aeschylus. No; I'll expose this crutch-and-cripple playwright,
And what he's worth, for all his insolence.

Dionysus [to attendants]. A lamb, a black lamb, quick,
boys! Bring it out
To sacrifice; a hurricane's let loose!

Aeschylus [to Euripides]. You and your Cretan dancing-
solos! You
And the ugly amours that you set to verse!

Dionysus [interposing]. One moment, please, most noble
Aeschylus!
And you, poor wretch, if you have any prudence,
Get out of the hailstones quick, or else, by Zeus,
Some word as big as your head will catch you crash
Behind the ear, and knock out all the . . . Telephus!
Nay, Aeschylus, pray, pray control your anger;
Examine and submit to be examined
With a cool head. Two poets should not meet
In fishwife style; but here are you, straight off,
Ablaze and roaring like an oak on fire.

Euripides. For my part I'm quite ready, with no shrinking,
To bite first or be bitten, as he pleases.
Here are my dialogue, music and construction;
Here's Peleus at your service, Meleager,
And Aeolus, and . . . yes, Telephus, by all means!

Dionysus. Do you consent to the trial, Aeschylus? Speak.

Aeschylus. I well might take objection to the place;
It's no fair field for him and me.

Dionysus.   Why not?

Aeschylus. Because my writings haven't died with me,
As his have; so he'll have them all to hand. . . .
However, I waive the point, if you think fit.

Dionysus. Go, some one, bring me frankincense and fire
That I may pray for guidance, to decide

This contest in the Muses' strictest ways;
To whom, meantime, uplift your hymn of praise!
Chorus [*while preparations are made for the sacrifice*].
   All hail, ye nine heaven-born virginal Muses,
   Whiche'er of ye watch o'er the manners and uses
      Of the Founts of Quotation, when, meeting in fray—
   All hearts drawn tense for who wins and who loses—
   With wrestling lithe each the other confuses,
      Look on the pair that do battle to-day!
   These be the men to take poems apart
      By chopping, riving, sawing;
   Here is the ultimate trial of Art
      To due completion drawing!
Dionysus. Won't you two pray before you show your
         lines?
Aeschylus [*going up to the altar*]. Demeter, thou who
         feedest all my thought,
   Grant me but worthiness to worship thee!
Dionysus [*to Euripides*]. Won't you put on some frankin-
         cense?
Euripides [*staying where he is*].   Oh, thank you;
   The gods I pray to are of other metal!
Dionysus. Your own stamp, eh?   New struck?
Euripides   Exactly so.
Dionysus. Well, pray away then to your own peculiar.
Euripides. Ether, whereon I batten!   Vocal chords!
   Reason, and nostrils swift to scent and sneer,
   Grant that I duly probe each word I hear.
Chorus.   All of us to hear are yearning
         Further from these twins of learning,
         What dread road they walk, what burning
            Heights they climb of speech and song
         Tongues alert for battle savage,
         Tempers keen for war and ravage,

Angered hearts to both belong.
He will fight with passes witty,
Smooth and smacking of the city,
    Gleaming blades unflecked with rust;
He will seize—to end the matter—
Tree-trunks torn and clubbed, to batter
Brains to bits, and plunge and scatter
    Whole arena-fulls of dust!

*[Dionysus is now seated on a throne as judge.
The poets stand on either side before him.]*

Dionysus. Now, quick to work. Be sure you both do
        justice to your cases,
    Clear sense, no loose analogies, and no long common-
        places.

Euripides. A little later I will treat my own artistic mettle,
    This person's claims I should prefer immediately to
        settle.
    I'll show you how he posed and prosed; with what
        audacious fooling
    He tricked an audience fresh and green from Phryni-
        chus's schooling.
    Those sole veiled figures on the stage were first among
        his graces,
    Achilles, say, or Niobe, who never showed their faces,
    But stood like so much scene-painting, and never a grunt
        they uttered!

Dionysus. Why, no, by Zeus, no more they did!

Euripides.   And on the Chorus spluttered
    Through long song-systems, four on end, the actors
        mute as fishes!

Dionysus. I somehow loved that silence, though; and felt
        it met my wishes
    As no one's talk does nowadays!

Euripides.   You hadn't yet seen through it!

D

That's all.

Dionysus.   I really think you're right! But still, what
made him do it?

Euripides. The instinct of a charlatan, to keep the audience
guessing
If Niobe ever meant to speak—the play meantime
progressing!

Dionysus. Of course it was!   The sly old dog, to think of
how he tricked us!—
Don't [*to Aeschylus*] ramp and fume!

Euripides [*excusing Aeschylus*].   We're apt to do so when
the facts convict us!
—Then after this tomfoolery, the heroine, feeling calmer,
Would utter some twelve wild-bull words, on mid-way
in the drama,
Long ones, with crests and beetling brows, and gorgons
round the border,
That no man ever heard on earth.

Aeschylus.   The red plague . . .!

Dionysus.   Order, order!

Euripides. Intelligible—not one line!

Dionysus [*to Aeschylus*].   Please! Won't your teeth
stop gnashing?

Euripides. All fosses and Scamander-beds, and bloody
targes flashing,
With gryphon-eagles bronze-embossed, and crags, and
riders reeling,
Which somehow never quite joined on.

Dionysus.   By Zeus, sir, quite my feeling!
A question comes in Night's long hours, that haunts
me like a spectre,
What kind of fish or fowl you'd call a " russet hippalector."

Aeschylus [*breaking in*]. It was a ship's sign, idiot, such as
every joiner fixes!

Dionysus. Indeed! I thought perhaps it meant that music-
man Eryxis!

Euripides. You like then, in a tragic play, a cock? You
think it mixes?

Aeschylus [to Euripides]. And what did you yourself
produce, O fool with pride deluded?

Euripides. Not " hippalectors," thank the Lord, nor
" tragelaphs," as you did—

The sort of ornament they used to fill a Persian
curtain!

—I had the Drama straight from you, all bloated and
uncertain,

Weighed down with rich and heavy words, puffed out
past comprehension.

I took the case in hand; applied treatment for such
distension—

Beetroot, light phrases, little walks, hot book-juice, and
cold reasoning;

Then fed her up on solos . . .

Dionysus [aside]. With Cephisophon for seasoning!

Euripides. I didn't rave at random, or plunge in and make
confusions.

My first appearing character explained, with due allusions,
The whole play's pedigree.

Dionysus [aside]. Your own you left in wise obscurity!

Euripides. Then no one from the start with me could
idle with security.

They had to work. The men, the slaves, the women,
all made speeches,

The kings, the little girls, the hags . . . .

Aeschylus. Just see the things he teaches!

And shouldn't you be hanged for that?

Euripides. No, by the lord Apollo!

It's democratic!

Dionysus [to Euripides]. That's no road for you, my friend,
        to follow;
    You'll find the 'little walk' too steep; I recommend
        you quit it.
Euripides. Next, I taught all the town to talk with freedom.
Aeschylus.   I admit it.
    'Twere better, ere you taught them, you had died amid
        their curses!
Euripides. I gave them canons to apply and squares for
        marking verses;
    Taught them to see, think, understand, to scheme for
        what they wanted,
    To fall in love, think evil, question all things . . .
Aeschylus.   Granted, granted!
Euripides. I put things on the stage that came from daily
        life and business,
    Where men could catch me if I tripped; could listen
        without dizziness
    To things they knew, and judge my art. I never
        crashed and lightened
    And bullied people's senses out; nor tried to keep
        them frightened
    With Magic Swans and Aethiop knights, loud barb and
        clanging visor!
    Then look at my disciples, too, and mark what creatures
        his are!
    Phormisius is his product and the looby lump
        Megainetus,
    All trumpet, lance, moustache, and glare, who twist
        their clubs of pine at us;
    While Cleitophon is mine, sirs, and Theramenes the
        Matchless!
Dionysus. Theramenes! Ah, that's the man! All danger
        leaves him scratchless.

His friends may come to grief, and he be found in awkward
    fixes,
But always tumbles right end up, not aces—no: all sixes!
Euripides. This was the kind of lore I brought
  To school my town in ways of thought;
  I mingled reasoning with my art
  And shrewdness, till I fired their heart
  To brood, to think things through and through;
  And rule their houses better, too.
Dionysus. Yes, by the powers, that's very true!
  No burgher now, who comes indoors,
  But straight looks round the house and roars:
  "Where is the saucepan gone?   And who
    Has bitten that sprat's head away?
  And, out, alas! The earthen pot
  I bought last year, is not, is not!
    Where are the leeks of yesterday?
    And who has gnawed this olive, pray?"
  Whereas, before they took his school,
  Each sat at home, a simple, cool,
  Religious, unsuspecting fool,
    And happy in his sheep-like way!

Chorus. Great Achilles, gaze around thee!
  'Twill astound thee and confound thee.
  Answer now: but keep in bound the
    Words that off the course would tear,
  Bit in teeth, in turmoil flocking.
  Yes: it's monstrous—shameful—shocking—

    Brave old warrior.   But beware!
  Don't retort with haste or passion;
  Meet the squalls in sailor fashion,
    Mainsail reefed and mast nigh bare;

Then, when safe beyond disaster,
You may press him fiercer, faster,
Close and show yourself his master,
    Once the wind is smooth and fair!

Dionysus. O thou who first of the Greeks did build great words to heaven-high towers,
And the essence of tragedy-padding distilled, give vent to thy pent-up showers.
Aeschylus. I freely admit that I take it amiss, and I think my anger is just,
At having to answer a man like this. Still, lest I should seem nonplussed,
Pray, tell me on what particular ground a poet should claim admiration?
Euripides. If his art is true, and his counsel sound; and if he brings help to the nation,
By making men better in some respect.
Aeschylus.   And suppose you have done the reverse,
And have had upon good strong men the effect of making them weaker and worse,
What, do you say, should your recompense be?
Dionysus.   The gallows! You needn't ask him.
Aeschylus. Well, think what they were when he had them from me! Good six-footers, solid of limb,
Well-born, well-bred, not ready to fly from obeying their country's call,
Nor in latter-day fashion to loiter and lie, and keep their consciences small;
Their life was in shafts of ash and of elm, in bright plumes fluttering wide,
In lance and greaves and corslet and helm, and hearts of seven-fold hide!

Euripides [*aside*]. Oh, now he's begun and will probably
   run a whole armourer's shop on my head!
[*To Aeschylus*] Stop! How was it due in especial to you,
   if they were so very—well-bred?
Dionysus. Come, answer him, Aeschylus! Don't be so hot,
   or smoulder in silent disdain.
Aeschylus [*crushingly*]. By a tragedy 'brimming with Ares!'
Dionysus.   A what?
Aeschylus.   The "Seven against Thebes."
Dionysus.   Pray explain.
Aeschylus. There wasn't a man could see that play but he
   hungered for havoc and gore.
Dionysus. I'm afraid that tells in the opposite way. For
   the Thebans profited more,
It urged them to fight without flinching or fear, and
   they did so; and long may you rue it!
Aeschylus. The same thing was open to all of you here, but
   it didn't amuse you to do it!
Then next I taught you for glory to long, and against
   all odds stand fast;
That was "The Persians," which bodied in song the
   noblest deed of the past.
Dionysus. Yes, yes! When Darius arose from the grave it
   gave me genuine joy,
And the Chorus stood with its arms a-wave, and observed,
   "Yow—oy, Yow—oy!"
Aeschylus. Yes, that's the effect for a play to produce! For
   observe, from the world's first start
Those poets have all been of practical use who have
   been supreme in their art.
First, Orpheus withheld us from bloodshed impure,
   and vouchsafed us the great revelation;
Musaeus was next, with wisdom to cure diseases and
   teach divination

Then Hesiod showed us the season to plough, to sow,
    and to reap.   And the laurels
That shine upon Homer's celestial brow are equally
    due to his morals!
He taught men to stand, to march, and to arm . . .
Dionysus.   So that was old Homer's profession?
Then I wish he could keep his successors from harm,
    like Pantacles in the procession,
Who first got his helmet well strapped on his head,
    and then tried to put in the plume!
Aeschylus. There be many brave men that he fashioned and
    bred, like Lamachus, now in his tomb.
And in his great spirit my plays had a part, with their
    heroes many and brave—
Teucers, Patrocluses, lions at heart; who made my
    citizens crave
To dash like them at the face of the foe, and leap at the
    call of a trumpet!—
But no Stheneboia I've given you, no; no Phaedra, no
    heroine-strumpet!
If I've once put a woman in love in one act of one play,
    may my teaching be scouted!
Euripides. No, you hadn't exactly the style to attract
    Aphrodite!
Aeschylus.   I'm better without it.
A deal too much of that style she found in some of your
    friends and you,
And once, at the least, left you flat on the ground!
Dionysus.   By Zeus, that's perfectly true.
If he dealt his neighbours such rattling blows, we must
    think how he suffered in person.
Euripides. And what are the public defects you suppose my
    poor Stheneboia to worsen?
Aeschylus [*evading the question with a jest*]. She makes good

women, and good men's wives, when their
hearts are weary and want ease,
Drink jorums of hemlock and finish their lives, to gratify
Bellerophontes!

Euripides. But did I invent the story I told of—Phaedra,
say? Wasn't it history?

Aeschylus. It was true, right enough; but the poet should
hold such a truth enveloped in mystery,
And not represent it or make it a play. It's his duty
to teach, and you know it.
As a child learns from all who may come in his way,
so the grown world learns from the poet.
Oh, words of good counsel should flow from his voice . . .

Euripides. And words like Mount Lycabettus
Or Parnes, such as you give us for choice, must needs
be good counsel?—Oh, let us,
Oh, let us at least use the language of men!

Aeschylus. Flat cavil, sir! cavil absurd!
When the subject is great and the sentiment, then, of
necessity, great grows the word;
When heroes give range to their hearts, is it strange if
the speech of them over us towers?
Nay, the garb of them too must be gorgeous to view,
and majestical, nothing like ours.
All this I saw, and established as law, till you came and
spoilt it.

Euripides. How so?

Aeschylus. You wrapped them in rags from old beggarmen's
bags, to express their heroical woe,
And reduce the spectator to tears of compassion!

Euripides. Well, what was the harm if I did?

Aeschylus [*evading the question as before*]. Bah, your modern
rich man has adopted the fashion, for remission
of taxes to bid;

" He couldn't provide a trireme if he tried "; he implores
us his state to behold.
Dionysus. Though rags outside may very well hide good
woollens beneath, if it's cold!
And when once he's exempted, he gaily departs and
pops up at the Fishmongers' stalls.
Aeschylus [*continuing*]. Then, next, you have trained in the
speechmaking arts nigh every infant that crawls.
Oh, this is the thing that such havoc has wrought in the
wrestling-school, narrowed the hips
Of the poor pale chattering children, and taught the
crews of the pick of the ships
To answer back pat to their officer's nose!   How unlike
my old sailor of yore,
With no thought in his head but to guzzle his brose
and sing as he bent at the oar!
Dionysus. And spit on the heads of the rowers below, and
garotte stray lubbers on shore!
But our new man just sails where it happens to blow, and
argues, and rows no more!
Aeschylus. What hasn't he done that is under the sun,
And the love-dealing dames that with him have begun ?
One's her own brother's wife;
One says Life is not Life;
And one goes into shrines to give birth to a son!
Our city through him is filled to the brim
With monkeys who chatter to every one's whim;
Little scriveners' clerks
With their winks and their larks,
But for wrestle or race not a muscle in trim!
Dionysus. Not a doubt of it!   Why, I laughed fit to cry
At the Panathenaea, a man to espy,
Pale, flabby, and fat,
And bent double at that,

Puffing feebly behind, with a tear in his eye;
Till there in their place, with cord and with brace,
Were the Potters assembled to quicken his pace;
    And down they came, whack!
    On sides, belly, and back,
Till he blew out his torch and just fled from the race!

Chorus.   Never were such warriors, never
        Prize so rich and feud so keen:
    Dangerous too, such knots to sever:
    He drives on with stern endeavour,
    He falls back, but rallies ever,
        Marks his spot and stabs it clean!

    Change your step, though!   Do not tarry;
    Other ways there be to harry
        Old antagonists in art.
    Show whatever sparks you carry,
    Question, answer, thrust and parry—
    Be they new or ancient, marry,
        Let them fly, well-winged and smart!

    If you fear, from former cases,
        That the audience p'raps may fail
    To appreciate your paces,
    Your allusions and your graces,
    Look a moment in their faces!
        They will tell another tale.

    Oft from long campaigns returning
    Thro' the devious roads of learning
        These have wandered, books in hand:

Nature gave them keen discerning
Eyes; and you have set them burning!
Sharpest thought or deepest yearning—
Speak, and these will understand.

Euripides. Quite so; I'll turn then to his Prologues straight,
And make in that first part of tragedy
My first review in detail of this Genius!
His exposition always was obscure.
Dionysus. Which one will you examine?
Euripides.   Which? Oh, lots!
First quote me that from the "Oresteia," please.
Dionysus. Ho, silence in the court! Speak, Aeschylus.
Aeschylus [*quoting the first lines of the "Choephoroi"*].
"Guide of the Dead, warding a father's way,
Be thou my light and saviour, where I pray,
In this my fatherland, returned, restored."
Dionysus [*to Euripides*]. You find some false lines there?
Euripides.   About a dozen!
Dionysus. Why, altogether there are only three!
Euripides. But every one has twenty faults in drawing!
                          [*Aeschylus begins to interrupt.*]
Dionysus. No, stop, stop, Aeschylus; or perhaps you'll find
Your debts run up to more than three iambics.
Aeschylus [*raging*]. Stop to let *him* speak?
Dionysus.   Well, that's my advice.
Euripides. He's gone straight off some thousand miles
                          astray.
Aeschylus. Of course it's foolery—but what do *I* care?
Point out the faults.
Euripides.   Repeat the lines again.
Aeschylus. "Guide of the Dead, warding a father's way . . ."
Euripides. Orestes speaks those words, I take it, standing
On his dead father's tomb?

Aeschylus.   I don't deny it.

Euripides. Then what's the father's way that Hermes wards?
Is it the way Orestes' father went,
To darkness by a woman's dark intent?

Aeschylus. No, no! He calls on Eriounian Hermes,
Guide of the Dead, and adds a word to say
That office is derived from Hermes' father.

Euripides. That's worse than I supposed! For if your Hermes
Derives his care of dead men from his father, . . .

Dionysus [*interrupting.*] Why, resurrectioning's the family
trade!

Aeschylus. Dionysus, dull of fragrance is thy wine!

Dionysus. Well, say the next; and [*to Euripides*] you look
out for slips.

Aeschylus. " Be thou my light and saviour where I pray
In this my fatherland returned, restored."

Euripides. Our noble Aeschylus repeats himself.

Dionysus. How so ?

Euripides.   Observe his phrasing, and you'll see.
First to this land " returned " and then " restored ";
" Returned " is just the same thing as " restored."

Dionysus. Why, yes! It's just as if you asked your neighbour,
" Lend me a pail, or, if not that, a bucket."

Aeschylus. Oh, too much talking has bemuzzed your brain!
The words are not the same; the line is perfect.

Dionysus. Now, is it really? Tell me how you mean.

Aeschylus. Returning home is the act of any person
Who has a home; he comes back, nothing more;
An exile both returns and is restored!

Dionysus. True, by Apollo! [*To Euripides*] What do you
say to that?

Euripides. I don't admit Orestes was restored.
He came in secret with no legal permit.

Dionysus. By Hermes, yes! [*Aside*] I wonder what they mean!

Euripides. Go on then to the next.   [*Aeschylus is silent.*]
Dionysus.   Come, Aeschylus,
    Do as he says: [*to Euripides*] and you look out for
            faults.
Aeschylus. " Yea, on this bank of death, I call my lord
    To hear and list. . . ."
Euripides.   Another repetition!
    " To hear and list "—the same thing palpably!
Dionysus. The man was talking to the dead, you dog,
    Who are always called three times—and then don't
            hear.
Aeschylus. Come, how did *you* write prologues ?
Euripides.   Oh, I'll show you.
    And if you find there any repetitions
    Or any irrelevant padding,—spit upon me!
Dionysus. Oh, do begin.   I mustn't miss those prologues
    In all their exquisite exactitude!
Euripides. " At first was Oedipus in happy state."
Aeschylus. He wasn't!   He was born and bred in misery.
    Did not Apollo doom him still unborn
    To slay his father ? . . .
Dionysus [*aside*].   His poor unborn father?
Aeschylus. " A happy state at first," you call it, do you?
Euripides [*contemptuously resuming*]. " At first was Oedipus
                in happy state,
    Then changed he, and became most desolate."
Aeschylus. He didn't.   He was never anything else!
    Why, he was scarcely born when they exposed him
    In winter, in a pot, that he might never
    Grow up and be his father's murderer.
    Then off he crawled to Polybus with sore feet,
    Then married an old woman, twice his age,
    Who further chanced to be his mother, then
    Tore out his eyes: the lucky dog he was!

Dionysus. At least he fought no sea-fight with a colleague
  Called Erasinides!
Euripides.   That's no criticism.
  I write my prologues singularly well!
Aeschylus. By Zeus, I won't go pecking word by word
  At every phrase; I'll take one old umbrella,[1]
  God helping me, and smash your prologues whole!
Euripides. Umbrellas to my prologues?
Aeschylus.   One umbrella!
  You write them so that nothing comes amiss,
  The bed-quilt, or the umbrella, or the clothes-bag,
  All suit your tragic verse!   Wait and I'll prove it.
Euripides. You'll prove it?   Really!
Aeschylus.   Yes.
Dionysus.   Begin to quote.
Euripides. " Aegyptus, so the tale is spread afar,
  With fifty youths fled in a sea-borne car,
  But, reaching Argos . . ."
Aeschylus.   Found his umbrella gone!
Dionysus. What's that about the umbrella!   Drat the thing!
  Quote him another prologue, and let's see.
Euripides. " Dionysus, who with wand and fawn-skin dight
  On great Parnassus races in the light
  Of leaping brands . . ."
Aeschylus.   Found *his* umbrella gone!
Dionysus. Alas! again the umbrella finds our heart!
Euripides [*beginning to reflect anxiously*]. Oh, it won't come
              to much, though!   Here's another,
  With not a crack to stick the umbrella through!
  " No man hath bliss in full and flawless health;
  Lo, this one hath high race, but little wealth;

---

[1] In his latest edition, Professor Murray has substituted the more
literal rendering ' oil-can.' With his permission, I have ventured to
go back to his original ' umbrella.' In consequence, metrical reasons
have compelled me to revert to the earlier edition in some places.

That, base in blood . . ."
Aeschylus.   Found his umbrella gone!
Dionysus. Euripides!
Euripides.   Well?
Dionysus.   Better furl your sails;
    The great umbrella bellies in the wind!
Euripides. Bah, I disdain to give a thought to it!
    I'll dash it from his hands in half a minute.

                              [*He racks his memory.*]
Dionysus. Well, quote another;—and avoid umbrellas.
Euripides. "From Sidon sailing forth, Agenor's son,
    Cadmus, long since . . ."
Aeschylus.   Found *his* umbrella gone!
Dionysus. Oh, this is awful!   Buy the thing outright,
    Before it riddles every blessed prologue!
Euripides. I buy him off?
Dionysus.   I strongly recommend it.
Euripides. No; I have many prologues yet to cite
    Where he can't find a chink for his umbrella.
    "As rapid wheels to Pisa bore him on,
    Pelops the Great . . ."
Aeschylus.   Found *his* umbrella gone!
Dionysus. What did I tell you?   There it sticks again!
    You might let Pelops have a new one, though—
    You get quite good ones very cheap just now.
Euripides. By Zeus, not yet! I still have plenty left.
    "Oineus from earth . . ."
Aeschylus.   Found *his* umbrella gone!
Euripides. You *must* first let me quote one line entire!
    "Oineus from earth a goodly harvest won,
    But, while he prayed, . . ."
Aeschylus.   Found his umbrella gone!
Dionysus. During the prayers!   Who can have been the
            thief?

Euripides [*desperately*]. Oh, let him be!   I defy him answer
          this—
   " Great Zeus in heaven, the word of truth has flown. . .
Dionysus. O mercy!   *His* is certain to be gone!
   They bristle with umbrellas hedgehog-wise,
   Your prologues: they're as bunged up as your eyes!
   For God's sake change the subject.—Take his songs!
Euripides. Songs?   Yes, I have materials to show
   How bad his are, and always all alike.

Chorus.   What in the world shall we look for next?
          Aeschylus' music!   I feel perplexed
            How he can want it mended.
          I have always held that never a man
          Had written or sung since the world began
            Melodies half so splendid!
          (Can he really find a mistake
            In the master of inspiration?
            I feel some consternation
          For our Bacchic prince's sake!)

Euripides. Wonderful songs they are!   You'll see directly;
   I'll run them all together into one.
Dionysus. I'll take some pebbles, then, and count for you.
Euripides [*singing*]. " O Phthian Achilles, canst hark to the
          battle's man-slaying shock,
      Yea, shock, and not to succour come?
   Lo, we of the Mere give worship to Hermes, the fount
          of our stock,
      Yea, shock, and not to succour come! "
Dionysus.   Two shocks to you, Aeschylus, there!
Euripides. " Thou choice of Achaia, wide-ruling Atrides,
          give heed to my schooling!
      Yea, shock, and not to succour come."

E

Dionysus.   A third shock that, I declare!

Euripides. " Ah, peace, and give ear!   For the Bee-Maids
            be near to ope wide Artemis' portals.
      Yea, shock-a-nock a-succour come!
   Behold, it is mine to sing of the sign of the way fate-
            laden to mortals;
         Yah, shocker-knocker succucum! "

Dionysus. O Zeus Almighty, what a chain of shocks!
   I think I'll go away and take a bath;
      The shocks are too much for my nerves and kidneys!

Euripides. Not till you've heard another little set
   Compounded from his various cithara-songs.

Dionysus. Well then, proceed; but don't put any shocks
            in!

Euripides. " How the might twin-throned of Achaia for
            Hellene chivalry bringeth
         Flattothrat toflattothrat!
   The prince of the powers of storm, the Sphinx thereover
            he wingeth
         Flattothrat toflattothrat!
   With deedful hand and lance the furious fowl of the air
         Flattothrat toflattothrat!
   That the wild wind-walking hounds unhindered tear
         Flattothrat toflattothrat!
   And War toward Aias leaned his weight,
         Flattothrat toflattothrat! "

Dionysus. What's Flattothrat?   Was it from Marathon
   You gathered this wool-gatherer's stuff, or where ?

Aeschylus. Clean was the place I found them, clean the place
   I brought them, loath to glean with Phrynichus
   The same enchanted meadow of the Muse.
   But any place will do for *him* to poach,
   Drink-ditties of Melêtus, Carian pipings,
   And wakes, and dancing songs.—Here, let me show you!

Ho, some one bring my lyre! But no; what need
Of lyres for this stuff? Where's the wench that plays
The bones?—Approach, Euripidean Muse,
These songs are meet for your accompaniment!

Dionysus. This Muse was once . . . no Lesbian; not at
all!

Aeschylus [*singing*]. " Ye halcyons by the dancing sea
Who babble everlastingly,
While on your bathing pinions fall
The dewy foam-sprays, fresh and free;
And, oh, ye spiders deft to crawl
In many a chink of roof and wall,
While left and right, before, behind,
Your fingers wi-i-i-ind
The treasures of the labouring loom,
Fruit of the shuttle's minstrel mind,
Where many a songful dolphin trips
To lead the dark-blue-beakéd ships,
And tosses with aërial touch
Temples and race-courses and such.
O bright grape tendril's essence pure,
Wine to sweep care from human lips;
Grant me, O child, one arm-pressure! " [*Breaking off.*]
That foot, you see?

Dionysus. I do.

Aeschylus. And he ?

Euripides. Of course I see the foot!

Aeschylus. And this is the stuff to trial you bring
And face my songs with the kind of thing
That a man might sing When he dances a fling
To mad Cyrênê's flute!
There, that's your choral stuff! But I've not finished,
I want to show the spirit of his solos!

[*Sings again ; mysteriously.*]

" What vision of dreaming,
　　Thou fire-hearted Night,
　Death's minion dark-gleaming,
　　Hast thou sent in thy might?
And his soul was no soul, and the Murk was his mother,
　a horror to sight!

　　Black dead was his robe, and his eyes
　　　All blood, and the claws of him great;
　　Ye maidens, strike fire and arise;
　　　Take pails to the well by the gate,
Yea, bring me a cruse of hot water, to wash off this
　vision of fate.

　　　Thou sprite of the Sea,
　　　　It is e'en as I feared!
　　　Fellow-lodgers of me,
　　　　What dread thing hath appeared?
Lo, Glykê hath stolen my cock, and away from the
　neighbourhood cleared!   [*Wildly.*]
　　　(Ye Nymphs of the Mountain give aid!
　　　And what's come to the scullery-maid ?)
　　　　　　　　　　　　　　　　[*Tearfully.*]
　　　And I—ah, would I were dead!—
　　　　To my work had given my mind;
　　　A spindle heavy with thread
　　　　My hands did wi-i-i-ind,
And I meant to go early to market, a suitable buyer
　to find!   [*Almost weeping.*]
　　　—But he rose, rose in the air
　　　On quivering blades of flight;
　　　He left me care, care;
　　　And tears, tears of despair,
　　　Fell, fell, and dimmed my sight!
　　　　[*Recovering himself; in florid, tragic style.*]

Children of Ida's snows,
Cretans, take up your bows,
And ring the house with many a leaping limb!
And thou, fair maid of bliss,
Dictynna, Artemis,
Range with thy bandogs through each corner dim;
Yea, Thou of twofold Fires,
Grant me my deep desires,
Thou Zeus-born Hecate; in all men's eyes
Let the detective sheen
Flashed from thy torches keen,
Light me to Glykê's house, and that lost fowl surprise!'

Dionysus. Come, stop the singing!
Aeschylus.   I've had quite enough!
What I want, is to bring him to the balance;
The one sure test of what our art is worth!
Dionysus. So that's my business next? Come forward, please;
I'll weigh out poetry like so much cheese!

A large pair of scales is brought forward, while the Chorus sing.

Chorus. Oh, the workings of genius are keen and laborious!
Here's a new wonder, incredible, glorious!
Who but this twain Have the boldness of brain
'To so quaint an invention to run?
Such a marvellous thing, if another had said it had
Happened to him, I should never have credited;
I should have just Thought that he must
Simply be talking for fun!

Dionysus. Come take your places by the balance.
Aeschylus and Euripides. There!
Dionysus. Now, each take hold of it, and speak your verse,

And don't let go until I say " Cuckoo."
Aeschylus and Euripides [*taking their stand at either side of
     the balance*]. We have it.
Dionysus.   Now, each a verse into the scale!
Euripides [*quoting the first verse of his " Medea "*].
   " Would God no Argo e'er had winged the brine."
Aeschylus [*quoting his " Philoctetes "*]. " Spercheios, and ye
     haunts of grazing kine! "
Dionysus. Cuckoo!   Let go.—Ah, down comes Aeschylus
   Far lower.
Euripides.   Why, what can be the explanation?
Dionysus. That river he put in, to wet his wares
   The way wool-dealers do, and make them heavier!
   Besides, you know the verse you gave had wings!
Aeschylus. Well, let him speak another and we'll see.
Dionysus. Take hold again then.
Aeschylus and Euripides.   There you are.
Dionysus.   Now speak.
Euripides [*quoting his "Antigone "*]. " Persuasion, save in
     speech, no temple hath."
Aeschylus [*quoting his " Niobe "*]. " Lo, one god craves no
     offering, even Death."
Dionysus. Let go, let go!
Euripides.   Why, his goes down again!
Dionysus. He put in Death, a monstrous heavy thing!
Euripides. But my Persuasion made a lovely line!
Dionysus. Persuasion has no bulk and not much weight.
   Do look about you for some ponderous line
   To force the scale down, something large and strong.
Euripides. Where have I such a thing, now?   Where?
Dionysus [*mischievously quoting some unknown play of Euri-
     pides*].   I'll tell you;
   " Achilles has two aces and a four! "—
[*Aloud*] Come speak your lines; this is the final bout.

Euripides [*quoting his " Meleager "*]. " A mace of weighted
    iron his right hand sped."
Aeschylus [*quoting his " Glaucus "*]. " Chariot on chariot lay,
    dead piled on dead."
Dionysus [*as the scale turns*]. He beats you this time too!
Euripides.   How does he do it?
Dionysus. Two chariots and two corpses in the scale—
  Why, ten Egyptians couldn't lift so much!
Aeschylus [*breaking out*]. Come, no more line-for-lines!
      Let him jump in
  And sit in the scale himself, with all his books,
  His wife, his children, his Cephisophon!
  I'll back two lines of mine against the lot!

The central door opens and Pluto with his suite comes forth

A Voice. Room for the King!
Pluto [*to Dionysus*].   Well, is the strife decided?
Dionysus [*to Pluto*]. I won't decide! The men are both my
    friends;
  Why should I make an enemy of either?
  The one's so good, and I so love the other!
Pluto. In that case you must give up all you came for!
Dionysus. And if I do decide?
Pluto.   Why, not to make
  Your trouble fruitless, you may take away
  Whichever you decide for.
Dionysus.   Hearty thanks!
  Now, both approach, and I'll explain.—I came
  Down here to fetch a poet: " Why a poet? "
  That his advice may guide the City true
  And so keep up my worship! Consequently,
  I'll take whichever seems the best adviser
  Advise me first of Alcibiades,
  Whose birth gives travail still to mother Athens

Pluto. What is her disposition towards him ?

Dionysus   Well,
   She loves and hates, and longs still to possess.
   I want the views of both upon that question!

Euripides. Out on the burgher, who to serve his state
   Is slow, but swift to do her deadly hate,
   With much wit for himself, and none for her.

Dionysus. Good, by Poseidon, that!—And what say you?
                                          [*To Aeschylus.*]

Aeschylus. No lion's whelp within thy precincts raise;
   But, if it *be* there, bend thee to its ways!

Dionysus. By Zeus the Saviour, still I can't decide!
   The one so fine, and the other so convincing!
   Well, I must ask you both for one more judgment;
   What steps do you advise to save our country?

Euripides. I know and am prepared to say!

Dionysus.   Say on.

Euripides. Where Mistrust now has sway, put Trust to
            dwell,
   And where Trust is, Mistrust; and all is well.

Dionysus. I don't quite follow.   Please say that again,
   Not quite so cleverly and rather plainer.

Euripides. If we count all the men whom now we trust,
   Suspect; and call on those whom now we spurn
   To serve us, we may find deliverance yet.

Dionysus. And what say you?

Aeschylus.   First tell me about the City;
   What servants does she choose?   The good?

Dionysus.   Great Heavens,
   She loathes them!

Aeschylus.   And takes pleasure in the vile?

Dionysus. Not she, but has perforce to let them serve her!

Aeschylus. What hope of comfort is there for a city
   That quarrels with her silk and hates her hodden ?

Dionysus. That's just what *you* must answer, if you want
  To rise again!
Aeschylus.　　　I'll answer there, not here.
Dionysus. No; better send up blessing from below.
Aeschylus. Her safety is to count her enemy's land
  Her own, yea, and her own her enemy's;
  Her ships her treasures, and her treasure dross!
Dionysus. Good;—though it all goes down the juror's throat!
Pluto [*interrupting*]. Come, give your judgment!
Dionysus.　　　　　　Well, I'll judge like this;
  My choice shall fall on him my soul desires!
Euripides. Remember all the gods by whom you swore
  To take me home with you, and choose your friend!
Dionysus. My tongue hath sworn;—but I'll choose
  　　　　　　Aeschylus!
Euripides. What have you done, you traitor?
Dionysus.　　　　　　　　I? I've judged
  That Aeschylus gets the prize. Why shouldn't I?
Euripides. Canst meet mine eyes, fresh from thy deed of
  shame?
Dionysus. What is shame, that the . . . Theatre deems
  no shame?
Euripides. Hard heart! You mean to leave your old friend
  dead?
Dionysus. Who knoweth if to live is but to die? . . .
  If breath is bread and sleep a woolly lie?
Pluto. Come in, then, both.
Dionysus.　　　　　　Again?
Pluto.　　　　　　　　To feast with me
  Before you sail.
Dionysus.　　　With pleasure! That's the way
  Duly to crown a well-contented day!
　　　　　　　[*They all depart into the house.*]

Chorus.   O blessed are they who possess
  An extra share of brains!
'Tis a fact that more or less
All fortunes of men express;
  As now, by showing
  An intellect glowing,

  This man his home regains;
Brings benefit far and near
To all who may hold him dear,
And staunches his country's tear,—
  All because of his brains.

  Then never with Socrates
  Make one of the row of fools
Who gabble away at ease,
Letting art and music freeze,
  And freely neglect
  In every respect
  The drama's principal rules!
Oh, to sit in a gloomy herd
A-scraping of word on word,
All idle and all absurd,—
  That is the fate of fools!

---

*Re-enter Pluto, Dionysus, Aeschylus, and Attendants, who
join with the Chorus to form a procession.*

Pluto. Then farewell, Aeschylus! Go your ways,
And save your town for happier days
By counsel wise; and a school prepare
For all the fools—there are plenty there!
And take me some parcels, I pray; this sword
Is for Cleophon; these pretty ropes for the Board

Of Providers.   But ask them one halter to spare
For Nicomachus; one, too, is Myrmex's share.
    And, along with this venomous
    Draught for Archenomus,
      Take them my confident prayer,

That they all will come here for a visit, and stay
And bid them be quick; for, should they delay,
Or meet my request with ingratitude, say
    I will fetch them myself, by Apollo!
And hurry the gang of them down with a run
All branded and chained—with Leucolophus' son
    The sublime Adimantus to follow!

Aeschylus. I will do as you wish.—And as for my throne,
    I beg you let Sophocles sit there alone,
    On guard, till perchance I return some day;
    For he—all present may mark what I say—
      Is my second in art and in wit.
    And see, above all, that this Devil-may-care
    Child of deceit with his mountebank air
    Shall never on that imperial chair
      By the wildest of accidents sit!

Pluto. With holy torches in high display
    Light ye the Marchers' triumphal advance;
    Let Aeschylus' music on Aeschylus' way
    Echo in song and in dance!

Chorus. Peace go with him and joy in his journeying!
      Guide ye our poet
    Forth to the light, ye Powers that reign in the Earth and
      below it;
    Send good thoughts with him, too, for the aid of a travail-
      ing nation,

So shall we rest at the last, and forget our long desolation,
War and the clashing of wrong.—And for Cleophon,
    why, if he'd rather,
Let him fight all alone with his friends, in the far-off
    fields of his father.
    [*They all go off in a procession, escorting Aeschylus.*

GILBERT MURRAY.

NOTES ON ARISTOPHANES' *FROGS*

[I have confined my attention in these notes to points which throw light on the history of Greek literature and on Greek literary criticism. I have not dealt with political allusions: nor have I indicated casual parodies of various lines from Greek tragedy.]

P. 4. *Son o' the goddess of the Greens.* Aristophanes constantly taunts Euripides with being the son of a green-groceress. The story is generally discredited by modern scholars.

P. 5. *Crutch-and-cripple playwright.* A reference to the famous *Telephus*, produced in 438, in which the hero appeared as a lame beggar.

Cretan dancing-solos. Euripides wrote two plays about Crete, both on unpleasant subjects. He considerably developed the solo song, which had been used to a less degree by his predecessors.

My writings haven't died with me. Aeschylus' plays, as a special honour, continued being acted after his death. Otherwise, plays were normally only performed once at Athens.

P. 7. *Phrynichus.* An elder contemporary of Aeschylus, and the first great figure of Athenian drama. Very little of him survives, but that little contains one lovely line.

Sole veiled figures. According to ancient authorities thi was a favourite device of Aeschylus. Niobe, they say, mourning for her children, kept silence for a third of the play. In the *Myrmidons*, Achilles sat silent and unbending while the chorus besought him to go out and fight. In the *Phrygians*, he listened in silence to Priam's prayer for the restitution of Hector's corpse.

Long song-systems. In point of fact, Aeschylus reduced the length of the choral portion: but it was still further reduced by his successors.

P. 8. *Twelve wild-bull words.* The extant remains of Aeschylus illustrate his fondness for long compounds.

"*Russet hippalector.*" In the *Myrmidons*, a lost play, the Trojans have set fire to the Greek fleet. The chorus, in an extant fragment, call attention to the melted paint running from a fantastic figure-head, representing a brown "horse-cock" ("hippalector"). This lapse from the sublime to the ridiculous was, we are told, a favourite theme of the comic poets. "Tragelaph" ("goat-stag") is another hybrid.

P. 9. *Cephisophon.* A friend of Euripides, credited by report with assisting him in composition.

The whole play's pedigree. Euripides liked to begin with a formal prologue, giving the events leading up to the action. (For examples see pp. 21–3 below.) Aeschylus preferred a more dramatic type of prologue; he sometimes, as Sophocles almost invariably did, started the play with a dialogue. The Euripidean type of prologue may in part be explained by his adoption of unfamiliar stories: but probably an abstract love of lucidity was the chief reason.

All made speeches. This is quite true. In Aeschylus, the minor characters talk: in Euripides, they frequently hold forth, sometimes with small regard for dramatic fitness.

P. 10. *No road for you to follow.* Euripides ended his days at the Court of Archelaus, King of Macedon.

P. 14. *Stheneboia.* She plays the part of Potiphar's wife in the *Bellerophon*, a lost play. Phaedra's guilty passion for her stepson is the theme of the extant *Hippolytus.*

P. 19. *Our noble Aeschylus repeats himself.* The systematic study of language was beginning at this time in Athens. A professor from the island of Ceos, one Prodicus, was a specialist in distinguishing between apparent synonyms.

P. 21. *One old umbrella.* The Greek says "oil-flask," an object of universal use.

The point of this episode is that the openings of Euripides' rologues are all of one pattern, beginning with a proper name, and going on with a subordinate clause or two, the first full stop coming a few lines down, so that "found his umbrella gone" may be substituted for the first main clause. This is, in fact, the sort of structure that naturally crops up if one tries to tell a story succinctly in verse. (Verrall, in the *New Quarterly*, January 1909, draws a clever parallel with the openings of Tennyson's *Idylls of the King*.) As a matter of fact, Euripides took pains to avoid the danger, and Aristophanes has to hunt hard for examples. The eighteen extant tragedies only furnish one between them, and that one he uses.

P. 23. *O Phthian Achilles, etc.* The point here is the alleged monotony of Aeschylean lyric metre. However the line starts, it always comes back to the same rhythm at the end.

P. 24. *Flattothrat toflattothrat.* This represents the thrumming of the harp. The musical jokes are of course lost to us.

P. 25. *The wench that plays the bones.* In a recent play, *Hypsipyle*, Euripides had introduced a woman soothing her baby with a rattle.

Ye halcyons. This lyric is a cento of lines from various plays of Euripides, selected for their metrical peculiarities. " Wi-i-i-ind " represents a sort of cadenza sung on a single syllable (each syllable normally being sung on one note). " That foot " refers to one of the offending metrical " feet." But there also appears to be a humorous allusion to a foot of some character on the stage.

P. 26. *What vision.* An amazingly clever parody of Euripides in his melodramatic vein. Pathetic repetitions (" rose, rose," etc.) were a mannerism of Euripides.

P. 27. *Come take your places.* The point of this episode is the metrical lightness of the Euripidean iambic line as compared with the Aeschylean.

II. ANTIPHANES

How easy it is to write a Tragedy

(A fragment from Antiphanes' comedy *Poetry*)

FRAG. 191, in Vol. ii. of Kock's *Comicorum Atticorum Fragmenta.*

TRAGEDY'S a lucky business altogether! First of all,
the audience always knows the story even before they're
told it. The poet has only got to remind them. I just
say *Oedipus*: they know all the rest—father, Laius: mother,
Jocasta: daughters, sons, what's to happen to him, what
he's done. Again, if some one says *Alcmeon,* the very children
at once cry out, " He went mad and killed his mother:
in a minute Adrastus will come in a fury and go away again."
Then, when they've nothing more to say, and their dramatic
invention is utterly exhausted, up goes the machine,[1] as easy
as lifting a finger, and the audience are satisfied. We can't
do that, we have to invent everything: new names, all that
has happened before the beginning of the play, the present
situation, the denouement, the opening. If Chremes or
Pheidon [2] forgets any of this, he is hissed off: but Peleus and
Teucer may forget if they like.

(I have translated this into prose, but the original is of course
in verse, like all Greek drama, tragedy and comedy.)

[1] A mechanical device by means of which a god (the proverbial
deus ex machina) was exhibited above the heads of the human characters. For the use and abuse of the ' machine,' see Aristotle's
Poetics, c. 15 (p. 132 below). Euripides' use of the contrivance is
generally in accord with Aristotle's precept.
[2] Typical figures in comedy. Peleus and Teucer are typical figures
in tragedy.

37

III. PLATO

The Chain of Inspiration from Muse to Listener

ION 533-536.

Socrates. I perceive, Ion; and I will proceed to explain to you what I imagine to be the reason of this. The gift which you possess of speaking excellently about Homer is not an art, but, as I was just saying, an inspiration; there is a divinity moving you, like that contained in the stone which Euripides calls a magnet, but which is commonly known as the stone of Heraclea. This stone not only attracts iron rings, but also imparts to them a similar power of attracting other rings; and sometimes you may see a number of pieces of iron and rings suspended from one another so as to form quite a long chain; and all of them derive their power of suspension from the original stone. In like manner the Muse first of all inspires men herself; and from these inspired persons a chain of other persons is suspended, who take the inspiration. For all good poets, epic as well as lyric, compose their beautiful poems not by art, but because they are inspired and possessed. And as the Corybantian revellers when they dance are not in their right mind, so the lyric poets are not in their right mind when they are composing their beautiful strains: but when falling under the power of music and metre they are inspired and possessed; like Bacchic maidens who draw milk and honey from the rivers when they are under the influence of Dionysus but not when they are in their right mind. And the soul of the lyric poet does the same, as they them-

38

selves say; for they tell us that they bring songs from honeyed
fountains, culling them out of the gardens and dells of the
Muses; they, like the bees, winging their way from flower to
flower. And this is true. For the poet is a light and
winged and holy thing, and there is no invention in him
until he has been inspired and is out of his senses, and the
mind is no longer in him: when he has not attained to this
state, he is powerless and is unable to utter his oracles.
Many are the noble words in which poets speak concerning
the actions of men; but like yourself when speaking about
Homer, they do not speak of them by any rules of art:
they are simply inspired to utter that to which the Muse
impels them, and that only; and when inspired, one of them
will make dithyrambs, another hymns of praise, another
choral strains, another epic or iambic verses—and he who
is good at one is not good at any other kind of verse: for
not by art does the poet sing, but by power divine. Had he
learned by rules of art, he would have known how to speak
not of one theme only, but of all; and therefore God takes
away the minds of poets, and uses them as his ministers,
as he also uses diviners and holy prophets, in order that we
who hear them may know them to be speaking not of themselves who utter these priceless words in a state of uncon-
sciousness, but that God himself is the speaker, and that
through them he is conversing with us. And Tynnichus
the Chalcidian affords a striking instance of what I am saying: he wrote nothing that any one would care to remember
but the famous paean which is in every one's mouth, one of
the finest poems ever written, simply an invention of the
Muses, as he himself says. For in this way the God would
seem to indicate to us and not allow us to doubt that these
beautiful poems are not human, or the work of man, but
divine and the work of God; and that the poets are only
the interpreters of the Gods by whom they are severally

F

possessed.   Was not this the lesson which the God intended to teach when by the mouth of the worst of poets he sang the best of songs?   Am I not right, Ion?

Ion. Yes, indeed, Socrates, I feel that you are; for your words touch my soul, and I am persuaded that good poets by a divine inspiration interpret the things of the Gods to us.

Soc. And you rhapsodists are the interpreters of the poets?

Ion. There again you are right.

Soc. Then you are the interpreters of interpreters?

Ion. Precisely.

Soc. I wish you would frankly tell me, Ion, what I am going to ask of you: When you produce the greatest effect upon the audience in the recitation of some striking passage, such as the apparition of Odysseus leaping forth on the floor, recognised by the suitors and casting his arrows at his feet, or the description of Achilles rushing at Hector, or the sorrows of Andromache, Hecuba, or Priam,—are you in your right mind?   Are you not carried out of yourself, and does not your soul in an ecstasy seem to be among the persons or places of which you are speaking, whether they are in Ithaca or in Troy or whatever may be the scene of the poem?

Ion. That proof strikes home to me, Socrates.   For I must frankly confess that at the tale of pity my eyes are filled with tears, and when I speak of horrors, my hair stands on end and my heart throbs.

Soc. Well, Ion, and what are we to say of a man who at a sacrifice or festival, when he is dressed in holiday attire, and has golden crowns upon his head, of which nobody has robbed him, appears weeping or panic-stricken in the presence of more than twenty thousand friendly faces, when there is no one despoiling or wronging him;—is he in his right mind or is he not?

Ion. No indeed, Socrates, I must say that, strictly speaking, he is not in his right mind.

Soc. And are you aware that you produce similar effects on most of the spectators?

Ion. Only too well; for I look down upon them from the stage, and behold the various emotions of pity, wonder, sternness stamped upon their countenances when I am speaking: and I am obliged to give my very best attention to them; for if I make them cry I myself shall laugh, and if I make them laugh I myself shall cry when the time of payment arrives.

Soc. Do you know that the spectator is the last of the rings which, as I am saying, receive the power of the original magnet from one another? The rhapsode like yourself and the actor are intermediate links, and the poet himself is the first of them. Through all these the God sways the souls of men in any direction which he pleases, and makes one man hang down from another. Thus there is a vast chain of dancers and masters and under-masters of choruses, who are suspended, as if from the stone, at the side of the rings which hang down from the Muse. And every poet has some Muse from whom he is suspended, and by whom he is said to be possessed, which is nearly the same thing; for he is taken hold of. And from these first rings, which are the poets, depend others, some deriving their inspiration from Orpheus, others from Musaeus; but the greater number are possessed and held by Homer. Of whom, Ion, you are one, and are possessed by Homer; and when any one repeats the words of another poet you go to sleep, and know not what to say; but when any one recites a strain of Homer you wake up in a moment, and your soul leaps within you, and you have plenty to say; for not by art or knowledge about Homer do you say what you say, but by divine inspiration and by possession; just as the

Corybantian revellers too have a quick perception of that strain only which is appropriate to the God by whom they are possessed, and have plenty of dances and words for that, but take no heed of any other.   And you, Ion, when the name of Homer is mentioned have plenty to say, and have nothing to say of others.   You ask, "Why is this?" The answer is that you praise Homer not by art but by divine inspiration.

B. Jowett.

Higher and Lower Arts

Gorgias 501–505.

Socrates. Then I will proceed, and ask whether you also agree with me, and whether you think that I spoke the truth when I further said to Gorgias and Polus that cookery in my opinion is only an experience, and not an art at all; and that whereas medicine is an art, and attends to the nature and constitution of the patient, and has principles of action and reason in each case, cookery in attending upon pleasure never regards either the nature or reason of that pleasure to which she devotes herself, but goes straight to her end, nor ever considers or calculates anything, but works by experience and routine, and just preserves the recollection of what she has usually done when producing pleasure.   And first, I would have you consider whether I have proved what I was saying, and then whether there are not other similar processes which have to do with the soul—some of them processes of art, making a provision for the soul's highest interest—others despising the interest, and, as in the previous case, considering only the pleasure of the soul, and how this may be acquired, but not considering what pleasures are good or bad, and having no other aim but to afford gratification, whether good or bad. In my opinion, Callicles, there are such processes, and this is the sort of thing which I term flattery, whether concerned with the body or the soul, or whenever employed with a view to pleasure and without any consideration of good and evil. And now I wish that you would tell me whether you agree with us in this notion, or whether you differ.

Callicles. I do not differ; on the contrary, I agree; for in that way I shall soonest bring the argument to an end, and shall oblige my friend Gorgias.

Soc. And is this notion true of one soul, or of two or more?

Cal. Equally true of two or more.

Soc. Then a man may delight a whole assembly, and yet have no regard for their true interests?

Cal. Yes.

Soc. Can you tell me the pursuits which delight mankind —or rather, if you would prefer, let me ask, and do you answer, which of them belong to the pleasurable class, and which of them not? In the first place, what say you of flute-playing? Does not that appear to be an art which seeks only pleasure, Callicles, and thinks of nothing else?

Cal. I assent.

Soc. And is not the same true of all similar arts, as, for example, the art of playing the lyre at festivals?

Cal. Yes.

Soc. And what do you say of the choral art and of dithy-rambic poetry?—are not they of the same nature? Do you imagine that Cinesias the son of Meles cares about what will tend to the moral improvement of his hearers, or about what will give pleasure to the multitude?

Cal. There can be no mistake about Cinesias, Socrates.

Soc. And what do you say of his father, Meles the harp-player? Did he perform with any view to the good of his hearers? Could he be said to regard even their pleasure? For his singing was an infliction to his audience. And of harp-playing and dithyrambic poetry in general, what would you say? Have they not been invented wholly for the sake of pleasure?

Cal. That is my notion of them.

Soc. And as for the Muse of Tragedy, that solemn and august personage—what are her aspirations? Is all her aim and desire only to give pleasure to the spectators, or does she fight against them and refuse to speak of their pleasant vices, and willingly proclaim in word and song truths welcome and unwelcome?—which in your judgment is her character?

Cal. There can be no doubt, Socrates, that Tragedy has her face turned towards pleasure and the gratification of the audience.

Soc. And is not that the sort of thing, Callicles, which we were just now describing as flattery?

Cal. Quite true.

Soc. Well now, suppose that we strip all poetry of song and rhythm and metre, there will remain speech?

Cal. To be sure.

Soc. And this speech is addressed to a crowd of people?

Cal. Yes.

Soc. Then poetry is a sort of rhetoric?

Cal. True.

Soc. And do not the poets in the theatres seem to you to be rhetoricians?

Cal. Yes.

Soc. Then now we have discovered a sort of rhetoric which is addressed to a crowd of men, women, and children, freemen and slaves. And this is not much to our taste, for we have described it as having the nature of flattery.

Cal. Quite true.

Soc. Very good. And what do you say of that other rhetoric which addresses the Athenian assembly and the assemblies of freemen in other states? Do the rhetoricians appear to you always to aim at what is best, and do they seek to improve the citizens by their speeches, or are they too, like the rest of mankind, bent upon giving them pleasure, forgetting the public good in the thought of their own interest, playing with the people as with children, and trying to amuse them, but never considering whether they are better or worse for this?

Cal. I must distinguish. There are some who have a real care of the public in what they say, while others are such as you describe.

Soc. I am contented with the admission that rhetoric is of two sorts; one, which is mere flattery and disgraceful declamation; the other, which is noble and aims at the training and improvement of the souls of the citizens, and strives to say what is best, whether welcome or unwelcome, to the audience; but have you ever known such a rhetoric; or if you have, and can point out any rhetorician who is of this stamp, who is he?

Cal. But, indeed, I am afraid that I cannot tell you of any such among the orators who are at present living.

Soc. Well, then, can you mention any one of a former generation, who may be said to have improved the Athenians, who found them worse and made them better, from the day that he began to make speeches? for, indeed, I do not know of such a man.

Cal. What! did you never hear that Themistocles was a good man, and Cimon and Miltiades and Pericles, who is just lately dead, and whom you heard yourself?

Soc. Yes, Callicles, they were good men, if, as you said at first, true virtue consists only in the satisfaction of our own desires and those of others; but if not, and if, as we were afterwards compelled to acknowledge, the satisfaction of some desires makes us better, and of others, worse, and we ought to gratify the one and not the other, and there is an art in distinguishing them,—can you tell me of any of these statesmen who did distinguish them?

Cal. No, indeed, I cannot.

Soc. Yet surely, Callicles, if you look you will find such a one.   Suppose that we just calmly consider whether any of these was such as I have described.   Will not the good man, who says whatever he says with a view to the best, speak with a reference to some standard and not at random; just as all other artists, whether the painter, the builder, the shipwright, or any other, look all of them to their own work, and do not select and apply at random what they apply, but strive to give a definite form to it?   The artist disposes all things in order, and compels the one part to harmonise and accord with the other part, until he has constructed a regular and systematic whole; and this is true of all artists, and in the same way the trainers and physicians, of whom we spoke before, give order and regularity to the body: do you deny this?

Cal. No; I am ready to admit it.

Soc. Then the house in which order and regularity prevail is good; that in which there is disorder, evil?

Cal. Yes.

Soc. And the same is true of a ship?

Cal. Yes.

Soc. And the same may be said of the human body?

Cal. Yes.

Soc. And what would you say of the soul?   Will the good soul be that in which disorder is prevalent, or that in which there is harmony and order?

Cal. The latter follows from our previous admissions.

Soc. What is the name which is given to the effect of harmony and order in the body?

Cal. I suppose that you mean health and strength?

Soc. Yes, I do; and what is the name which you would give to the effect of harmony and order in the soul? Try and discover a name for this as well as for the other.

Cal. Why not give the name yourself, Socrates?

Soc. Well, if you had rather that I should, I will; and you shall say whether you agree with me, and if not, you shall refute and answer me. " Healthy," as I conceive, is the name which is given to the regular order of the body, whence comes health and every other bodily excellence: is that true or not?

Cal. True.

Soc. And " lawful " and " law " are the names which are given to the regular order and action of the soul, and these make men lawful and orderly:—and so we have temperance and justice: have we not?

Cal. Granted.

Soc. And will not the true rhetorician who is honest and understands his art have his eye fixed upon these, in all the words which he addresses to the souls of men, and in all his actions, both in what he gives and in what he takes away? Will not his aim be to implant justice in the souls of his citizens and take away injustice, to implant temperance and take away intemperance, to implant every virtue and take away every vice? Do you not agree?

Cal. I agree.

Soc. For what use is there, Callicles, in giving to the body of a sick man who is in a bad state of health a quantity of the most delightful food or drink or any other pleasant thing, which may be really as bad for him as if you gave him nothing, or even worse if rightly estimated? Is not that true?

Cal. I will not say No to it.

Soc. For in my opinion there is no profit in a man's life if his body is in an evil plight—in that case his life also is evil: am I not right?

Cal. Yes.

Soc. When a man is in health the physicians will generally allow him to eat when he is hungry and drink when he is thirsty, and to satisfy his desires as he likes, but when he is sick they hardly suffer him to satisfy his desires at all: even you will admit that?

Cal. Yes.

Soc. And does not the same argument hold of the soul, my good sir? While she is in a bad state and is senseless and intemperate and unjust and unholy, her desires ought to be controlled, and she ought to be prevented from doing anything which does not tend to her own improvement.

Cal. Yes.

Soc. Such treatment will be better for the soul herself?

Cal. To be sure.

Soc. And to restrain her from her appetites is to chastise her?

Cal. Yes.

Soc. Then restraint or chastisement is better for the soul than intemperance or the absence of control, which you were just now preferring?

B. Jowett.

The Madness of Poetry

Phaedrus 244.

The third kind is the madness of those who are possessed by the Muses; which taking hold of a delicate and virgin soul, and there inspiring frenzy, awakens lyrical and all other numbers; with these adorning the myriad actions of ancient heroes for the instruction of posterity. But he who, having no touch of the Muses' madness in his soul, comes to the door and thinks that he will get into the temple by the help of art—he, I say, and his poetry are not admitted; the sane man disappears and is nowhere when he enters into rivalry with the madman.

B. JOWETT.

Necessary Sequence a Mark of Good Writing

PHAEDRUS 264. (A speech of Lysias is under discussion.)

Socrates. Then as to the other topics—are they not thrown down anyhow? Is there any principle in them? Why should the next topic follow next in order, or any other topic? I cannot help fancying in my ignorance that he wrote off boldly just what came into his head, but I dare say that you would recognise a rhetorical necessity in the succession of the several parts of the composition?

Phaedrus. You have too good an opinion of me if you think that I have any such insight into his principles of composition.

Soc. At any rate, you will allow that every discourse ought to be a living creature, having a body of its own and a head and feet; there should be a middle, beginning, and an end, adapted to one another and to the whole?

Phaedr. Certainly.

Soc. Can this be said of the discourse of Lysias? See whether you can find any more connexion in his words than in the epitaph which is said by some to have been inscribed on the grave of Midas the Phrygian.

Phaedr. What is there remarkable in the epitaph?

Soc. It is as follows:—

> I am a maiden of bronze and lie on the tomb of Midas:
> So long as water flows and tall trees grow,
> So long here on this spot by his sad tomb abiding,
> I shall declare to passers-by that Midas sleeps below.

Now in this rhyme whether a line comes first or comes last, as you will perceive, makes no difference.

B. Jowett.

Knowledge of Technique is not Everything

Phaedrus 268–270.

Socrates. What power has this art of rhetoric, and when?

Phaedrus. A very great power in public meetings.

Soc. It has. But I should like to know whether you have the same feeling as I have about the rhetoricians? To me there seem to be a great many holes in their web.

Phaedr. Give an example.

Soc. I will. Suppose a person to come to your friend Eryximachus, or to his father Acumenus, and to say to him: "I know how to apply drugs which shall have either a heating or a cooling effect, and I can give a vomit and also a purge, and all that sort of thing; and knowing all this, as I do, I claim to be a physician and to make physicians by imparting this knowledge to others,"—what do you suppose that they would say?

Phaedr. They would be sure to ask him whether he knew "to whom" he would give his medicines, and "when," and "how much."

Soc. And suppose that he were to reply: "No; I know nothing of all that; I expect the patient who consults me to be able to do these things for himself"?

Phaedr. They would say in reply that he is a madman or a pedant who fancies that he is a physician because he has read something in a book, or has stumbled on a prescription or two, although he has no real understanding of the art of medicine.

Soc. And suppose a person were to come to Sophocles or Euripides and say that he knows how to make a very long speech about a small matter, and a short speech about a great matter, and also a sorrowful speech, or a terrible, or threatening speech, or any other kind of speech, and in teaching this fancies that he is teaching the art of tragedy—?

Phaedr. They too would surely laugh at him if he fancies that tragedy is anything but the arranging of these elements in a manner which will be suitable to one another and to the whole.

Soc. But I do not suppose that they would be rude or abusive to him: would they not treat him as a musician would a man who thinks that he is a harmonist because he knows how to pitch the highest and the lowest note; happening to meet such an one he would not say to him savagely, " Fool, you are mad! " But like a musician, in a gentle and harmonious tone of voice, he would answer: " My good friend, he who would be a harmonist must certainly know this, and yet he may understand nothing of harmony if he has not got beyond your stage of knowledge, for you only know the preliminaries of harmony and not harmony itself."

Phaedr. Very true.

Soc. And will not Sophocles say to the display of the would-be tragedian, that this is not tragedy but the preliminaries of tragedy? and will not Acumenus say the same of medicine to the would-be physician?

Phaedr. Quite true.

Soc. And if Adrastus the mellifluous or Pericles heard of these wonderful arts, brachyologies and eikonologies and all the hard names which we have been endeavouring to draw into the light of day, what would they say? Instead of losing temper and applying uncomplimentary epithets, as you and I have been doing, to the authors of such an imaginary art, their superior wisdom would rather censure us, as well as them. " Have a little patience, Phaedrus and Socrates, they would say; you should not be in such a passion with those who from some want of dialectical skill are unable to define the nature of rhetoric, and consequently suppose that they have found the art in the preliminary conditions of it, and when these have been taught by them to others, fancy that the whole art of rhetoric has been taught by them; but as to using the several instruments of the art effectively, or making the composition a whole,—an application of it such as this is they regard as an easy thing which their disciples may make for themselves."

Phaedr. I quite admit, Socrates, that the art of rhetoric which these men teach and of which they write is such as you describe—there I agree with you. But I still want to know where and how the true art of rhetoric and persuasion is to be acquired.

Soc. The perfection which is required of the finished orator is, or rather must be, like the perfection of anything else, partly given by nature, but may also be assisted by art. If you have the natural power, and add to it knowledge and practice, you will be a distinguished speaker; if you fall short in either of these, you will be to that extent defective. But the art, as far as there is an art, of rhetoric does not lie in the direction of Lysias or Thrasymachus.

Phaedr. In what direction then?

Soc. I conceive Pericles to have been the most accomplished of rhetoricians.

Phaedr. What of that?

Soc. All the great arts require discussion and high speculation about the truths of nature; hence come loftiness of thought and completeness of execution. And this, as I conceive, was the quality which, in addition to his natural gifts, Pericles acquired from his intercourse with Anaxagoras whom he happened to know. He was thus imbued with the higher philosophy, and attained the knowledge of Mind and the negative of Mind, which were favourite themes of Anaxagoras, and applied what suited his purpose to the art of speaking.

B. JOWETT.

The Imitative Element in Poetry and Music

REPUBLIC 392–402.

"Then that may suffice for the subject matter. We must now, I fancy, examine the question of diction, and then we shall have thoroughly examined both what the poets are to say and how they are to say it?"

Adeimantus said, "I don't understand what you mean by that."

"But we must see that you do," I said. "Perhaps you will grasp it better in this way. Is not everything which is said by story-tellers or poets a narration of past, present, or future events?"

"What else?" he said.

"Then do they not use either simple narration or imitative narration, or both?"

"That again," he said, "I need to have explained to me."

"I am evidently a ridiculously obscure teacher," I said. "But as poor speakers do, I shall leave the general principle alone, and taking a particular example try to make my meaning clear to you. You know the beginning of the *Iliad* where the poet says that Chryses asks Agamemnon to ransom his daughter and he angrily refuses, and then Chryses,

since his request is refused, prays to the god against the
Achaeans ? ”

" I do.”

" Well, you know that up to the lines:

> And made suit to all, but most to the commands
> Of both th' Atrides who most ruled,

the poet speaks in his own person, and does not try to make
us think that the speaker is any one but himself; but in
the passage after that he speaks as though he were himself
Chryses, and tries as hard as he can to make us think that
the speaker is not Homer, but the old priest.   And all the
rest of the narrative concerning the events in Ilium and in
Ithaca, and all the *Odyssey* is written in much the same way.”

" Certainly,” he said.

" And are not all those speeches and the parts between
the speeches equally narrative ? ”

" Surely.”

" But when he speaks in the person of another, shall we
not say that he then always makes his style as nearly as
possible like that of the man whom he has announced to
be speaking ? ”

" We shall, of course.”

" But if the man makes himself either in voice or in look
like another man, does he not imitate that man ? ”

" Of course.”

" Then in such cases, it appears, Homer and the other
poets carry on the narration by means of imitation ? ”

" Certainly.”

" Now if the poet never concealed his own person, his
whole poem and narration would be without imitation.
To prevent you from saying that you still don't understand,
I shall tell you how this would work out.   After Homer
has told how Chryses came bearing gifts to ransom his
daughter, and how he made supplication to the Achaeans,

and especially to the chiefs, if after that he had spoken, not
as if he had been transformed into Chryses, but as if he
were still Homer, that, you know, would not have been
imitation, but simple narration.   It would have gone in
some such way as this.   I shall not put it in metre, as I am
no poet.   The priest came and prayed that the gods might
grant to them the capture of Troy and a safe return, and
entreated them to ransom his daughter, taking the gifts he
offered in fear of the god.   And when he had spoken,
the others reverenced his words and gave assent;   but
Agamemnon was angry and told him to go away and not
to come back, or his sacred staff and the fillets of the god
would not protect him.   He said that Chryses' daughter
should grow old with him in Argos before he would ransom
her, and told Chryses to go away and to refrain from anger
if he wanted to get home safe.   The old man when he
heard this was afraid and went away in silence; but when
he left the army behind him, he prayed earnestly to Apollo,
calling on the god by his titles, and putting him in remem-
brance, and asking to be repaid if ever he had made him
an acceptable offering by building his temple or sacrificing
victims.   In return for these services, he prayed that the
Achaeans might be made to pay for his tears by the arrows
of the god.   Thus, my friend," I said, " it becomes simple
narration without imitation."

"I understand," he said.

"You will understand then," I said, "that we have the
opposite form to this, when the words of the poet between
the speeches are struck out, and only the alternating dialogue
is left."

"Yes," he said, "I understand.   That happens in
tragedy."

"Your supposition," I said, "is quite correct, and I
fancy that now I can make you see what before I could

G

not, namely that all poetry and story-telling may be said to be in one of three forms; the first where imitation is employed throughout is, as you suggest, tragedy and comedy; in the second, the poet tells his own story—the best example of that is perhaps the dithyramb; in the third, both imitation and simple narration are used—it is found in epic and in several other kinds of poetry. I hope that you follow me."

" Yes, I now understand what you meant."

" Then let me remind you that we have said before that we were agreed as to the proper subjects of poetry, but had still to consider its proper manner."

" Yes, I remember."

" Well, then, this is what I was trying to say, that we must come to an agreement as to whether we should allow our poets to make their narrations by means of imitation, or partly by imitation and partly by the other method, in which case we should have to determine where each method should be used, or whether we should forbid imitation altogether."

" I think," he said, " that you are considering whether we shall admit tragedy and comedy into the city or not."

" Possibly," I said, " but possibly even more than that. I don't myself know as yet. We must go where the wind of the argument carries us."

" Yes," he said, " you say well."

" Then, Adeimantus, consider whether our guardians ought to be imitative or not? Does not the answer follow from what we have said already, that each man can practise well one profession but not many, and that if he attempts more, and meddles with many, he will fail in all to attain creditable distinction? "

" That is certainly the case."

" Then will not the same argument apply to imitation?

The same man cannot imitate many things as well as one."

" No, certainly not."

" Then he will hardly be able to practise any worthy profession and at the same time imitate many things and be imitative, since as a matter of fact the same persons are not successful even in two forms of imitation that seem very closely allied, in writing tragedy and comedy, for example. Did you not describe these as forms of imitation? "

" I did, and you are right. The same writers are never successful in both."

" Nor can any one be both a rhapsodist and an actor with any success."

" True."

" We even find that tragedy and comedy cannot be played by the same actor. And all these are forms of imitation, are they not? "

" They are."

" Then, Adeimantus, human nature seems to me to be split up into even smaller subdivisions, so that a man is unable to imitate many things well, or to do well the things themselves of which the imitations are likenesses."

" That is perfectly true," he said.

" Then if we are to be faithful to our original position, that our guardians must be released from all other handicrafts to be in all earnestness craftsmen of the freedom of the city, and must do nothing that does not contribute to this end, then, as they are to do nothing else, they must certainly not imitate. And if they do, they must imitate from childhood subjects befitting their vocation, brave, temperate, pious, free men, and the like; but meanness and any other ugly thing they must neither do nor be able to imitate, lest from the imitation they become infected with the reality. Have you not noticed that the practice of imitation, if it is begun in youth and persisted in, leaves its impress upon character and nature, on body and voice and mind?"

"Yes, certainly," he said.

"Then we shall not allow persons for whom we say we care, and they men, and men who must grow up good, to imitate a woman, whether she be young or old, either railing at her husband, or striving and vaunting herself against the gods, thinking that she is happy, or overcome by misfortune, or grief, or tears; much less shall we allow them to imitate one who is ill, or in love, or in labour."

"Most certainly not," he said.

"Nor may they imitate slaves, male or female, doing servile actions."

"No, they may not."

"Nor, it would follow, may they imitate bad men or cowards, or men doing actions of the contrary nature to those we described, reviling and caricaturing one another, using abominable language, whether drunk or sober, or committing any other faults of speech or action characteristic of that class of men in their personal demeanour and their relations with others. I think, too, that they must not get into the habit of making themselves resemble madmen, either in word or action. They must know madmen and bad men and women, but they must neither do nor imitate any of their actions."

"Most true," he said.

"Further," I said, "may they imitate smiths or any other craftsmen at their trade, or men rowing in triremes or their boatswains, or anything else of that kind?"

"How should they," he said, "when they are not to be allowed even to pay attention to any of those things?"

"Then will they imitate horses neighing, and bulls

bellowing, and rivers gurgling, and seas crashing, and thunder, and all those things?"

"No," he said, "we have already forbidden them to be mad or to make themselves like madmen."

"Then," I said, "if I understand your meaning, there is one form of diction and narration which would be used by the truly noble and good man when he needed to say anything, and another different form which a man of the opposite nature and breeding would find congenial, and which he would use."

"What are these?" he said.

"The man of measured character in the first place, when he came in his narration to the speech or action of a good man, would, I think, wish to speak in the good man's person, and would not be ashamed of that kind of imitation. He would imitate the good man with especial thoroughness in his cautious and wise actions, less carefully and to a less degree when he was overcome by disease, or love, or by drunkenness, or any other misfortune. But when he comes to some one unworthy of him, he will not be willing to liken himself seriously to his inferior. He may for a little when he is doing a good action, but apart from that he will be ashamed, partly because he is not in the way of imitating such people, but also from a repugnance to moulding and conforming himself to the morals of inferior men whom he deliberately despises; unless it be for mere amusement."

"That is likely," he said.

"Then he will use the form of narration which we described a little while ago, which is used in Homer. His manner of speech will partake both of imitation and simple narration, and only a small part of the whole will be imitation. Am I not right?"

"Yes, certainly," he said, "such must be the model for such a speaker."

" Then," I said, " as for the man of a different character, the more contemptible he is, the more will he narrate everything without discrimination and think nothing beneath him, so that he will attempt in sober earnest, and before a large audience, to imitate everything, as we said a moment ago—thunder and the noise of the wind, and of hail, and of wheels and of pulleys; the notes of trumpets and flutes, and fifes and all manner of instruments; the barking of dogs and the bleating of sheep, and the cries of birds. And so his manner of speech will all involve imitation of voice and form, with possibly a little simple narration."

" Yes," he said, " that is inevitable."

" Then these," I said, " are the two classes of diction? "

" They are," he said.

" Then of the two, may we not say that the first involves no violent changes, and if it be given a musical mode and rhythm in accord with the diction, it may be performed correctly in almost the same mode throughout; that is, since its character is so uniform, in one musical mode, and also in a similarly unchanging rhythm? "

" Yes," he said, " that is certainly the case."

" Then what of the other kind?   Does it not require just the opposite for its proper expression, all musical modes and all different rhythms, so many and manifold are its transitions? "

" Yes, that is very true."

" Do not all poets and writers hit upon one or other of those modes of diction, or on a mixture of both? "

" That is inevitable," he said.

" What then shall we do? " I said.   " Shall we admit into our city all those different styles, or one or other of those primary styles, or the mixture? "

" If my opinion prevails," he said, " we shall admit the simple imitator of the good man."

" But, Adeimantus, the mixed style is certainly attractive, while the opposite style to that which you have chosen is much the most popular with children and their attendants, and with the vulgar mass."

" Popular it may be."

" But perhaps," I said, " you will say that it is not befitting in our city where no man is twofold or manifold, since each does his own work, and that only."

" No, it is not befitting."

" Therefore is this not the only city where we shall find the shoemaker actually a shoemaker, and not sea captain and maker of shoes in one; the farmer a farmer, and not adding jury work to his farming: and the soldier a soldier, and not money-maker and soldier in one, and so with them all?"

" True," he said.

" Then apparently if there come to our city a man so wise that he can turn into everything under the sun and imitate every conceivable object, when he offers to show off himself and his poems to us, we shall do obeisance to him as to a sacred, wonderful, and agreeable person; but we shall say that we have no such man in our city, and the law forbids there being one, and we shall anoint him with myrrh, and crown him with a wreath of sacred wool, and send him off to another city, and for ourselves we shall employ a more austere and less attractive poet and story-teller, whose poetry will be to our profit, who will imitate for us the diction of the good man, and in saying what he has to say will conform to those canons which we laid down originally when we were undertaking the task of educating the soldiers?"

" Yes," he said, " we shall do that, if it lie in our power."

" Here, then," I said, " we have apparently completely finished with that branch of music which relates to literature and stories. We have discovered both subject and manner."

" Yes, I think with you," he said.

" Then after that," I said, " we have left the manner and the melody of the singing."

" Obviously."

" Well, would not any one without further consideration see what we should have to say as to the proper nature of these elements, if we are to be consistent with what has gone before ? "

" Then, Socrates," said Glaucon, laughing, " I am apparently no one; for at this moment I can't infer with any assurance what kinds we ought to allow, though I have my suspicions."

" Well, in any case," I said, " you can at least say with assurance that a song is composed of three elements—words, musical mode, and rhythm."

" Yes," he said, " that is so."

" Well, as for the words, will they in any way differ from words that are not to go with music so far as concerns their conformity to those canons of subject and manner which we announced a little while ago? "

" No, they will not."

" And should not the musical mode and the rhythm accord with the words? "

" Of course."

" But we said that in our poems we want no weepings and lamentations."

" No, certainly not."

" What are the wailful modes? Tell me. You are musical."

" Mixed Lydian and Hyperlydian, and some other similar ones."

" Then these we must dismiss, must we not? " I said.

" For even in the training of virtuous women they are useless, much more so in the training of men."

" Certainly."

" Then are not drunkenness, effeminacy, and idleness most unseemly in guardians? "

" Surely."

" Which are the soft and convivial modes? "

" There are Ionian and Lydian modes which are called slack."

" Then, my friend, shall we use those for men who are warriors? "

" By no means," he said. " You seem to have Dorian and Phrygian left."

" I do not know these modes," I said; " but leave us the mode which will fittingly imitate the tones and accents of a man who is brave in battle and in every difficult and dangerous task, who, if he fails, or sees before him wounds or death, or falls into any other misfortune, always grapples with his fate, disciplined, and resolute. Another shall imitate a man in the actions of peace, where his choice has scope and he is free from compulsion; when he is persuading or entreating a god in prayer, or a man by instruction and advice, or when he is attending to the requests, or instruction, or persuasion of another. It shall imitate a man who in all these circumstances acts according to his liking, never puffing himself up, but in all his actions, and in his acceptance of their consequences, is ever prudent and restrained. These musical modes, two in number, one of compulsion, the other of free will, which imitate in the fairest manner the tones of the unfortunate and the fortunate, of the prudent and the brave, these you may leave to us."

" But," he said, " you are asking for just those which I mentioned a little while ago."

" Then," I said, " we shall not require for our songs

and melodies a variety of strings or sudden changes of modulation?"

"I think not," he said.

"Then we shall not maintain the makers of harps and dulcimers, and of all instruments which are many stringed and many keyed?"

"I think not."

"Then will you allow flute makers and flute players into the city? Has not the flute more notes than any other instrument, and are not those many-keyed instruments really imitations of the flute?"

"Obviously," he said.

"You have left," I said, "the lyre and the zither, which will be useful in town, and in the fields the herdsmen may have a pipe."

"So the argument tells us," he said.

"We are making no innovation," I said, "when we prefer Apollo and Apollo's instruments to Marsyas and his instruments."

"No, by Zeus," he said, "I think we are not."

"Now, by the dog," I said, "here have we been purging the city which we said before was too luxurious, and we never noticed it."

"Well, it was very wise of us," he said.

"Come, then," I said, "let us finish our purgation. After musical modes comes the canon of rhythm, according to which we must not aim at a variety of rhythms with all kinds of metrical feet, but must discover what are the rhythms of an orderly and brave life. When we have done so, we must make our metre and our melody to suit the words describing such a life, and not make words to suit metre and melody. Which these rhythms are, it is your business to tell us, as you told us of the musical modes."

"But, my good sir," he said, "I can't tell you. I

know that there are three kinds of rhythm from which the measures are woven, just as in tones I could on examination discover four kinds which are the basis of all musical modes. But which imitate which kind of life I can't tell you."

" Well," I said, " we shall consult Damon on this subject, and ask him which metrical feet are fitter to express meanness and pride, or madness or other evil, and which rhythms must be kept to express the opposite qualities. I fancy that I have heard him using the expressions 'warlike,' 'complex,' 'dactyl,' and 'heroic' of a rhythm. He arranged it in a way I do not understand, and showed the balance of the rise and fall of the feet as the rhythm passed from short to long, and I fancy that he called one foot an iambus and another a trochee, and assigned them longs and shorts. In some of them I think his praise and blame referred to the tempo of the separate foot as much as to the whole rhythm, or perhaps it was to the combined effect of both; I cannot say definitely. But these matters, as I said, we may leave to Damon, for to settle them would take a great deal of discussion; or do you think otherwise? "

" Not I, assuredly."

" But this you can settle, that grace and awkwardness accompany a good and a bad rhythm, can you not? "

" Surely."

" But goodness and badness of rhythm follow the diction. The good rhythm is assimilated to a beautiful style, and bad rhythm to the opposite; and so with goodness and badness of music, since, as we said, rhythm and musical mode conform to the words, not the words to them."

" Yes," he said, " they must follow the words."

" Then what of the style and the subject? Do they not conform to the character of the soul? "

" Surely."

" And the others conform to the style? "

" Yes."

" Then good speech and good music, and grace and good rhythm follow good nature, not that silliness which we call good nature in compliment, but the mind that is really well and nobly constituted in character."

" Most certainly," he said.

" Then if our young men are to do their own work, must they not follow after these? "

" They must."

" But painting and all craftsmanship are, we know, imbued with these; so are weaving and embroidery, architecture and the making of all other articles; so too is the body and other living things.   All these show either grace or absence of grace.   And absence of grace and bad rhythm and bad harmony are sisters to bad words and bad nature, while their opposites are sisters and copies of the opposite, a wise and good nature."

" That is certainly the case."

" Then we must speak to our poets and compel them to impress upon their poems only the image of the good, or not to make poetry in our city.   And we must speak to the other craftsmen and forbid them to leave the impress of that which is evil in character, unrestrained, mean and ugly, on their likenesses of living creatures, or their houses, or on anything else which they make.   He that cannot obey must not be allowed to ply his trade in our city.   For we would not have our guardians reared among images of evil as in a foul pasture, and there day by day and little by little gather many impressions from all that surrounds them, taking them all in until at last a great mass of evil gathers in their inmost souls, and they know it not.   No, we must seek out those craftsmen who have the happy gift of tracing out the nature of the fair and graceful, that our young men may dwell as in a health-giving region,

where all that surrounds them is beneficent, whencesoever
from fair works of art there smite upon their eyes and ears
an affluence like a wind bringing health from happy regions,
which, though they know it not, leads them from their
earliest years into likeness and friendship and harmony
with the principle of beauty."

"A nobler manner of education," he said, "there could
not be."

"Then, Glaucon," I said, "is not musical education of
paramount importance for those reasons, because rhythm
and harmony enter most powerfully into the innermost part
of the soul and lay forcible hands upon it, bearing grace
with them, so making graceful him who is rightly trained,
and him who is not, the reverse?   Is it not a further reason
that he who has been rightly trained in that city would be
quick to observe all works of art that were defective or
ugly, and all natural objects that failed in beauty?   They
would displease him, and rightly; but beautiful things he
would praise, and receiving them with joy into his soul
would be nourished by them and become noble and good.
Ugly things he would rightly condemn, and hate even in
his youth before he was capable of reason; but when reason
comes he would welcome her as one he knows, with whom
his training has made him familiar."

"Yes," he said, "I think that those are the purposes of
education in music."

"Now, in learning to read," I said, "we had become
fairly proficient by the time that we could recognise the
few letters that there are, in all the different words in which
they are scattered about: when we never passed them over,
either in a big word or a small, as though they were not
worth noticing, but were anxious to distinguish them
everywhere, knowing that we should be no scholars until
we had got thus far."

" True."

" Is it not also true that we shall not know the images of letters, supposing they are to be seen in water or in mirrors, before we know the letters themselves? The same skill and practice is needed in either case? "

" Most certainly."

" Then, by heaven, is it not true that in the same way neither we ourselves shall become musical, nor will the guardians whom we say we have to educate, until we can recognise the forms of temperance and courage and liberality and high-mindedness, and those which are akin to them, and also their opposites, wherever they are scattered about, until we discern them wherever they are to be found, both the forms and their images, never slighting them in big things or in small, but believing that the same skill and practice is needed to discern both form and image? "

A. D. LINDSAY.

The Theory of Poetry further Developed

REPUBLIC 595–608.

" There are a great many things about the city," I said, " which make me think in how extraordinarily sound a manner we have founded it; but I feel this most especially when I think about poetry."

" To what do you refer? " he said.

" To our refusal to admit all imitative poetry. Now that we have distinguished the different elements of the soul, it appears, I think, to be more obvious than ever that this refusal should be absolute."

" What do you mean? "

" Between ourselves—and don't denounce me to the tragic poets and all the other imitators—all such things seem to pollute the understanding of those who hear them, unless they possess a knowledge of their real nature; that is an antidote."

"What makes you say this?" he said.

"It must be uttered," I answered, "though a certain love and reverence for Homer which I have had from my childhood would forbid my speaking. For surely of all those noble tragic poets he is the master and the leader. Still I must not honour a man more than I honour truth, but must utter what I have to say."

"Yes, certainly," he said.

"Then listen, or rather answer."

"Ask your question."

"Could you tell me the general nature of imitation? For I don't myself quite understand what it sets out to be."

"Then it is likely, is it not, that I shall understand?" he said.

"There would be nothing out of the way if you did," I answered. "Dull eyes have often beaten sharp ones."

"So they have," he said. "But if I had any opinion, I should not be at all eager to express it in your presence. So do you consider yourself."

"Shall we begin the inquiry according to our ordinary method? We have been in the habit, if you remember, of positing a Form, wherever we use the same name in many instances, one Form for each 'many.' Do you understand?"

"I do."

"And shall we take whatever 'many' you please? For example, if this will do, there are many beds and tables."

"Surely."

"But for these articles there are two Forms, one of a bed and one of a table?"

"Yes."

"And have we not also been in the habit of saying, that

it is by looking at the Form that the manufacturer of each article makes the beds or the tables which we use, and so with other things? For no manufacturer manufactures the actual Form, does he?"

"Certainly not."

"Now consider this manufacturer. What would you call him?"

"Whom?"

"He who by himself makes all things which are made by all the different craftsmen."

"A marvellous clever fellow!"

"Wait a little, and you will soon say that with more reason. For this same craftsman is not only able to make all manufactured articles, but he makes all things that grow from the earth and fashions all living creatures, himself with the rest of them, and, not content with that, fashions earth and heaven, and gods and all things in heaven, or in Hades under the earth."

"What a perfectly marvellous genius," he said.

"Do you not believe me?" I asked. "Tell me. Do you think there is no such manufacturer at all, or do you think that a man might be in a certain manner a maker of all these things and in another manner not? Don't you see that you yourself could make all these things in a certain manner?"

"And what is that manner?" he said.

"It is not hard," I answered, "but a frequent and easy mode of manufacture. It is most easily done perhaps if you take a mirror and turn it round to all sides. You will soon make a sun and stars, the earth, yourself, and other living creatures, manufactured articles and plants, and everything we have just described."

"Yes," he said, "make them in appearance, but surely not as they are in truth."

" Your remark is excellent," I answered, " and just what
the argument wants.   For the painter also, I imagine, is
one of these manufacturers.   Is he not ? "

" Surely."

" But you will say, I fancy, that what he makes, he does
not make truly.   Though the painter also makes a bed in
a manner, does he not ? "

" Yes," he said, " he, like the other, makes a bed in
appearance."

" What of the carpenter ?   But did you not say that he
makes, not the Form which we asserted to be that which
a bed is, but a particular bed ? "

" Yes, I said so."

" Now, if he does not make what is, he will not make
the real, but something which is of the same nature with
but is not the real.   And if any one were to say that the
work of the carpenter or of any other craftsman was perfectly real, he would probably not be speaking the truth,
would he ? "

" No," he said, " at least not in the opinion of persons
acquainted with this kind of reasoning."

" Then let us not be surprised if the manufactured
article is also somewhat indistinct as compared with truth."

" No."

" Shall we then," I said, " take these as examples in our
search after the nature of the imitator ? "

" If you please," he said.

" Now there are these three beds, first the bed which
exists in nature, which we should say, I fancy, was made
by God.   Should we not ? "

" By God, I fancy."

" And one made by the carpenter ? "

" Yes," he said.

" And one made by the painter ? "

H

" Yes, let us suppose so."

" Painter, carpenter, and God, these three are set over the three classes of beds."

" Yes, these three."

" And God, whether because he so willed or because there was some necessity upon him not to make more than one bed in nature, made that one which is the reality of a bed and only that. But two or more such beds were never produced by God, and never will be."

" How is that?" he said.

" Because," I answered, " if God should make even no more than two, then yet another would be revealed whose Form the first two would express, and this, and not the two, would be the reality of a bed."

" You are right," he said.

" And God, I imagine, knew this, and wished to be really maker of a bed that really was and not only a particular manufacturer of a particular bed, and therefore produced this one natural bed."

" Probably."

" Then shall we call him the ' nature maker' of this thing, or something of that kind?"

" Yes, that is only just," he said, " when his making of this and all other things is nature's making of them."

" What of the carpenter? Do you call him a manufacturer of a bed?"

" Yes."

" And you call the painter also a manufacturer and maker of the same kind of thing?"

" Certainly not."

" Then what is he of a bed?"

" I think," he answered, " that he would be most fairly described as an imitator of what the other two manufacture."

"Good," I said. "You call him an imitator who is concerned with that which is begotten three removes from nature?"

"Certainly," he said.

"And the tragedian, since he is an imitator, will be then one whose nature is third from the king and from the truth, and all the other imitators will be like him?"

"That seems probable."

"Then we are agreed as to the imitator. But tell me this about the painter. Do you think that he tries to imitate each reality in nature, or the works of the manufacturers?"

"The works of the manufacturers," he said.

"To imitate them as they are, or as they appear? You must make this further distinction."

"What do you mean?" he said.

"This. Does a bed really differ from itself when you look at it from the side or from straight in front or from any other point of view, or does it remain the same but appear different? And so with other things."

"The second alternative is right," he said. "It appears, but is not different."

"Now consider this point. Which of these two governs the drawing of any subject? Is drawing an attempt to imitate the real as it is, or the appearance as it appears? Is it an imitation of an appearance or of a truth?"

"Of an appearance," he said.

"Imitation, then, is far from the truth, and apparently it manages to make all things just because it attacks only a small part of each, and that an image. The painter, for example, will paint us, we say, a shoemaker, a carpenter, and all other workmen, though he has no knowledge whatever of their crafts. But nevertheless, if he is a good painter, he may paint a carpenter and show the thing at some distance, and so cheat children and stupid men into thinking it is really a carpenter."

" Surely."

" Well, my friend, I imagine that we must come to this conclusion about all these matters. When any one announces to us that he has met a man who knows all handicrafts, and who of all the things known by each separate individual has a more exact knowledge than any of them, to such a person we must reply that he is more or less of a fool, and has apparently met with a wizard and imitator, and been cheated into thinking the man possessed of unusual wisdom, all because he could not distinguish knowledge and lack of knowledge and imitation."

" Very true," he said.

" And after this," I said, " we must examine tragedy, and Homer its leader, since people tell us that tragedians know all arts and all things human that relate to virtue and vice and things divine. For a good poet, they say, if he is to make a beautiful poem on his subject, must do so with knowledge of that subject, or fail altogether. We must then inquire whether these persons have met with the imitators and been cheated, and, on seeing their productions, have failed to perceive that they are three removes from being, and can easily be made without knowledge of the truth—for their productions are appearances and not realities—or whether there is something in what they say, and good poets really have knowledge of those subjects of which their descriptions are approved by common opinion."

" Yes," he said, " this must certainly be investigated."

" Now, do you suppose that if any man could make both the object of imitation and the image, that he would trouble to set himself down to the manufacture of images, and would put this power in the forefront of his life as his best possession ? "

" Not I."

" But, I imagine, if he had true knowledge of those things which he also imitates, he would be much more zealous in the doing than in the imitation of them, and would try to leave many beautiful deeds as memorials behind him. He would much rather be the hero whose praises are sung than the poet who sings them."

" I think so," he answered. " The honour and benefit are far greater."

" Well, on other questions we may give up the idea of calling Homer, or any other poet, to account, by asking whether any of them had medical knowledge, and was not merely an imitator of medical discourses; where are the people whom any poet, ancient or modern, is said to have restored to health, as Asclepius did; what students of medicine they have left behind them to match the descendants of Asclepius. And so with the other arts we may refrain from such questions, and let be. But when Homer tries to tell of the mightiest and most noble things, of wars and generalship and government of cities and the education of man, then it is only fair we should question him, and inquire, ' My dear Homer, if, as you say, you are not thrice removed from truth concerning virtue, a manufacturer of an image, and what we have called an imitator; if you are but twice removed, and can know what practices make men better individuals and better citizens, can you not mention a city to which you gave a better government, as Lycurgus gave to Lacedaemon, and many other persons to many cities great and small? Does any city name you a good lawgiver and its benefactor? So Italy and Sicily name Charondas, and we Solon. Who so names you?' Will he be able to mention one?"

" I think not," said Glaucon. " Why, even the devotees of Homer don't say that."

" But is there an account of any war in that time which was well waged under the command or advice of Homer? "

" No."

" Well, is there mention of many inventions, contrivances of use in handicrafts or in any other branch of action, which would show that he was a clever practical man, like Thales of Miletus, or Anacharsis the Scythian? "

" No, nothing of the kind."

" Well, if there is no mention of public services, do we hear that Homer in his lifetime was guide and educator to certain individuals, who loved him for the inspiration of his society, and who handed down to those who came after them a Homeric way of life? Such was Pythagoras. For that master was greatly loved for such reasons, and his successors even up to the present day talk of the Pythagorean manner of life, and seem somehow to be quite distinct from other people."

" No," he said, " we do not hear of anything of that kind. For if the stories about Homer are true, Socrates, his companion Creophylus would as an example of education be even funnier than his funny name. For they say that Homer was very much neglected in his lifetime, not to speak of what happened afterwards."

" Yes, so they say," I answered.   " But consider, Glaucon, if Homer had really been able to educate men and make them better, if he had attained not merely to imitation but to knowledge of these subjects, would he not have made many disciples and been honoured and loved by them? Why, Protagoras of Abdera and Prodicus of Ceos and many others can by their private intercourse inspire their followers with the belief that they will be unable to rule either their households or their city unless these masters superintend their education, and for this wisdom of theirs they are so devotedly loved, that their disciples almost insist on carrying them about shoulder high. Now if Homer had been able to help men to be virtuous, would the men of the time have allowed him and Hesiod to wander about singing their songs; would they not have laid hold of them as more precious than gold, and compelled them to dwell at home with them; or if they had not succeeded in that, would they not have taken the direction of their education into their own hands and followed them wherever they went until they had got adequate instruction?"

" I think, Socrates," he said, " that what you say is most certainly true."

" Then may we lay down that, beginning with Homer, all the poets are imitators of images of virtue and of all the other subjects on which they write, and do not lay hold of truth; rather, as we said a moment ago, the painter will produce what seems to be a shoemaker, though he himself have no understanding of shoemaking, and his spectators have none, but judge only by colour and form?"

" Certainly."

" And so, I imagine, we shall say that the poet also by means of words and sentences reproduces the colours, as it were, of the several arts, having only enough under-standing to imitate; and he too has his spectators who judge by words and think if any one in metre and rhythm and musical mode describes shoemaking or generalship or any other subject, that what is said is good. Such is the great magical power which these things possess. For when the works of the poets are stripped of the colours that music gives them, and are spoken simply and by themselves, I fancy that you know what they look like. I dare say you have noticed."

" I have," he said.

" Might we not compare them," I said, " to faces with the freshness of youth but without real beauty when they suffer change and have lost their early bloom?"

" Certainly," he replied.

" Come then, consider this. The maker of the image, the imitator, we say, has no understanding of what is, but only of what appears; is it not so ? "

" Yes."

" But let us not leave the question half stated, but consider it adequately."

" Speak on," he said.

" Will a painter, say, paint reins and bridle ? "

" Yes."

" But a saddler and a smith will make them ? "

" Certainly."

" Does the painter know what the reins and the bridle ought to be like ?   Or is it the case that not even the smith and the saddler, who made them, know that, but only the horseman, the man who knows how to use them ? "

" Very true."

" And shall we not say the same about everything ? "

" What ? "

" That there are three arts concerned with each thing— one that uses, one that makes, and one that imitates ? "

" Yes."

" Then are the virtue and beauty and correctness of every manufactured article and living creature and action determined by any other consideration than the use for which each is designed by art or nature ? "

" No."

" Then it is quite inevitable that the user of each thing should have most experience of it, and should be the person to inform the maker what are the good and bad points of the instrument as he uses it.   For example, the flute-player informs the flute-maker about the flutes which are to serve him in his fluting; he will prescribe how they ought to be made, and the maker will serve him."

" Surely."

" Then he who knows gives information about good and bad flutes, and the other will make them, relying on his statements? "

" Yes."

" Then the maker of any article will have a right belief concerning its beauty or badness, which he derives from his association with the knower, and from listening, as he is compelled to do, to what the knower says; but the user has knowledge? "

" Certainly."

" Now will the imitator have knowledge derived from use as to whether or not the subjects which he paints are beautiful and right, or will he have right belief derived from compulsory intercourse with the man who knows and from being told how he ought to depict them? "

" Neither."

" Then the imitator will neither know nor have right belief concerning the beauty or the defects of the subjects of his imitation? "

" Apparently not."

" Then the poetic imitator will be charming in his wisdom on the subjects of his poetry? "

" Not so very charming."

" For all that he will imitate without knowing wherein each thing is bad or good; but he will probably imitate what appears to be beautiful to ordinary and ignorant people? "

" Certainly."

" Then apparently we have come to a thorough agreement on this, that the imitative man has no knowledge of any value on the subjects of his imitation; that imitation is a form of amusement and not a serious occupation; and that those who write tragic poetry in iambics and hexameters are all imitators in the highest degree? "

" Certainly."

" By Zeus," I said, " is not this imitation concerned with something that is third from the truth? "

" Yes."

" And what is it in man on which it exercises such effect as it has? "

" What kind of thing do you mean? "

" Something of this sort. You know that the same magnitude seen from a distance and from near at hand does not appear to us to be the same? "

" No."

" And the same thing appears bent when seen in water and straight when taken out of it, or both concave and convex, owing to a perversion of the vision by colours, and there is quite evidently a general confusion on this matter in our soul. It is this affection of our nature on which drawing in perspective relies to try all its magic arts upon us, and so it is in jugglery, and many other similar contrivances."

" True."

" And have not measurement and counting and weighing been shown to render most charming assistance in these difficulties? For the rule in our minds of the apparently larger or smaller or more or heavier, they substitute the rule of that which has counted or measured, or, if you like, weighed? "

" Surely."

" And this will be the work of the reasoning element in the soul? "

" It will."

" But when this element has made its measurements several times, and announces of any two things that one is greater or less than the other, or that they are equal, you have opposite conclusions about the same things appearing simultaneously? "

" Yes."

" Now did we not say that it was impossible for the same element to come simultaneously to opposite conclusions about the same things?"

" We did, and rightly."

" Then that in the soul whose judgments disagree with the measurements, will not be the same as that whose judgments are in accordance with them?"

" No."

" But that which relies on calculation and measurement will be the best element in the soul?"

" Of course."

" Then that which opposes it will be one of the beggarly elements in us?"

" Inevitably."

" This was the point which I wanted to settle when I said that drawing and in fact all imitation produces its own work quite removed from truth, and also associates with that element in us which is removed from insight and is its companion, and is friend to no healthy or true purpose."

" Certainly," he answered.

" Then imitation is a beggar wedded to a beggar and producing beggarly children?"

" Apparently."

" Does this apply only to visual imitation," I asked, " or also to imitation by sound, which we call poetry?"

" Naturally to that also," he said.

" Well," I said, " let us not rely on the natural analogy in painting but turn to that actual element of the understanding with which poetic imitation associates and see whether it is bad or good."

" Yes, we must."

" Let us put it in this way.   Imitation, we say, imitates men acting compulsorily or voluntarily, thinking that in the event they have done well or ill, and throughout either feeling pain or rejoicing. Is there anything else besides that?"

" Nothing."

" Now in all this process, is a man in one and the same disposition of mind? Or just as in seeing he was in a state of dissension, and had in himself simultaneous and opposing beliefs about the same things, so likewise in conduct is he not also at dissension and war with himself? And I may remind you that there is no need for us now to come to an agreement on this; for in the previous discussion on all these points we came to an agreement that our soul is full of countless simultaneous oppositions of this kind."

" We were right," he said.

" We were," I answered. " But I think we must now discuss what we then omitted."

" What is that?" he said.

" We said at that time, if you remember," I answered, " that a reasonable man, if he meets with a misfortune, like the loss of a son or anything else which he holds very dear, will bear it much more easily than other people."

" Certainly."

" Now let us consider this point. Will he feel no sorrow at all; or if that is an impossibility, will he show some sort of moderation in his grief?"

" The second alternative is nearer the truth," he said.

" Now tell me this about him. Do you fancy that he will fight and contend with his grief better when he is under the observation of his fellows, or when he is alone by himself in solitude?"

" Much better," he said, " when he is under observation."

" Yes. When he is alone I imagine he will utter many

cries of which he would be ashamed if there were any one
to hear him, and do many things which he would not allow
any one to see him doing."

" That is so," he said.

" Now is not that which encourages him to resist, reason
and law, while that which draws him to his sufferings is
the affliction itself?"

" True."

" And since there is in the man impulsion in contrary
directions in regard to the same thing at the same time,
we must say that the impulsions are two."

" Surely."

" And the one is ready to obey the law and follow
its guidance?"

" Yes."

" Now the law says that it is best to take misfortunes as
quietly as possible and not to grieve, because the good and
evil in such matters are not certain, and to take them hardly
makes things no better for the future; because no human
affairs are worth taking very seriously; and, finally, because
grief is a hindrance to that state of mind to which we should
come in our troubles as quickly as possible."

" To what do you refer?" he asked.

" A man should take thought," I said, " on what has
come to pass, and as we regulate our play by the fall of the
dice, so he should regulate his affairs in the light of what
has fallen out, as reason ordains will be best. We should
not be like children who, when they have stumbled, go on
holding the injured part and shrieking, but should always
accustom the soul to turn as quickly as possible to the healing
and restoring of that which is fallen and diseased, making
lamentation to disappear before medicine."

" That certainly would be the most correct attitude to
misfortune," he said.

" Now the best part in us, we say, wishes to follow this reasoning."

" Obviously."

" Then shall we not say that that element which impels us to recall our affliction and to lament, and which can never have enough of such things, is unreasoning and idle and a lover of cowardice? "

" Yes, we shall."

" Now the one, the complaining element, lends itself to much and diverse imitation, but the prudent and quiet character, which is always at one with itself, is not easily imitated, nor when imitated is it easily understood, especially in crowded audiences when men of every character flock to the theatre. For them it is the imitation of a disposition with which they are not familiar."

" Certainly."

" Then obviously it is not this character in the soul towards which the imitative poet is by nature set, or which his wisdom is bent on pleasing, since he is to win a great reputation with the common people, but rather the peevish and diverse character, because it is such a good object of imitation? "

" Obviously."

" Then we may now justly lay hold of the poet and set him over against the painter; for he resembles him in producing what has little value for truth, and also in associating with a similar part of the soul, which is not the best. And so we may now with justice refuse to allow him entrance to a city which is to be well governed, because he arouses and fosters and strengthens this part of the soul and destroys the reasoning part. Like one who gives a city over into the hands of villains, and destroys the better citizens, so we shall say that the imitative poet likewise implants an evil constitution in the soul of each individual; he gratifies

the foolish element in it, that which cannot distinguish
between great and small but thinks that the same things
are sometimes great and sometimes small, and he manufactures images very far removed from the truth."

" Certainly."

" But we have not yet stated our mightiest accusation
against imitation. For its power of corrupting even the
good, all but a few, is surely most terrible of all."

" Surely, if it does actually do that."

" Listen and consider. Take the best of us listening to
Homer or any other of the tragic poets, when he is imitating
a hero in grief and spinning out a long melancholy lamentation or imitating men singing and disfiguring themselves in
grief: you know that he gives us pleasure, and we give
ourselves up to following him; we sympathise and are
seriously impressed, and praise as a good poet whoever most
affects us in this way."

" I know we do."

" But when an intimate sorrow comes to any of us, you
notice that we pride ourselves on the opposite kind of
behaviour, on being able to bear it with quiet and endurance,
as though this were playing a man's part, and the other
behaviour, which we then praised, were playing a woman's."

" Yes," he said.

" Then is the praise rightly given? " I asked. " Is it
right to look at a man being what we ourselves should not
wish to be without shame, and so far from feeling disgust, to
enjoy and praise the performance? "

" No, by Zeus," he said, " it does not seem reasonable."

" That is right," I said, " if you look at it in that way."

" In what way? "

" If you consider that the element, which in our own
intimate misfortunes is held down by force and stinted of
its fill of weeping and lamentation, those things which it

is its nature to desire, is the very part which the poets satisfy and please; while what by nature is best in us, for want of being adequately trained either by reason or by habit, relaxes its watch over the weeping element. The sorrows which it beholds are not its own, and if another man with pretensions to virtue grieve more than he might, there is no disgrace for it in praising and pitying him, but there is, it thinks, the actual profit of the pleasure, and therefore it will not consent to lose that pleasure by despising the whole poem. For it is given to few, I fancy, to reflect that other men's sorrows contribute to our own. For if we feed the element of pity on other's misfortunes and make it strong, it is not easy to control it in our own."

" Very true," he said.

" And does not the same argument apply to the humorous? You may take an extraordinary pleasure in hearing at a representation of comedy or in a circle of friends jests which you would be ashamed to make yourself, and will not hate them for their vileness; but are you not doing just what you did in tragic performances? It was by reason, again, that you held down that in you which wanted to jest, because you feared to be thought a buffoon, and now you let it free and pamper it at these performances, with the result that often you have quite unconsciously gone the length of being a comic poet in your own conduct? "

" Certainly," he said.

" And with regard to sexual desires, and anger, and all feelings of desire and pain and pleasure in the soul, which we say follow all our actions, you observe that poetic imitation produces all these effects in us. They should be withered, and it waters them and makes them grow. It makes them rule over us, when they ought to be subjects if we are to become better and happier, instead of worse and more miserable."

" I can't disagree with you," he said.

"Then, Glaucon," I said, "when you find Homer's admirers saying that this poet has educated Hellas, and that in questions of human conduct and culture a man ought to read and study Homer, and organise his whole life in accordance with the teaching of this poet, you must be friendly and kind to such people—they are as good as they know how to be—and agree that Homer is the most poetical and the first of the tragic poets, but be quite sure in your mind that only such specimens of poetry as are hymns to the gods or praises of good men are to be received into a city. If you receive the pleasure-seasoned Muse of song and epic, pleasure and pain will be kings in your city instead of law and the principle which at all times has been decided by the community to be the best."

"Very true," he said.

"Let it, then," I said, "be our defence now that we have recurred to the subject of poetry, that it was only to be expected that we should expel poetry from the city, such being her nature. The argument compelled us. And let us tell her also, in case she should accuse us of brutality and boorishness, that there is an ancient quarrel between philosophy and poetry. Phrases like ' the bitch that at her master yelps,' 'the yelping hound that in assemblies of the fools exalts its head,' 'the conquering rabble of the over-wise,' the statement that ' the men of subtle thought are beggars all,' and many others, are signs of this ancient antagonism. Nevertheless, let us state that if the pleasure-producing poetry and imitation have any arguments to show that she is in her right place in a well-governed city, we shall be very glad to receive her back again. We are conscious of the charm she exercises upon us. Only to betray the truth as it appears to us is impious. Do not you, my friend, also feel her magic charm, especially when she speaks with Homer's lips?'"

I

" Very much so."

" Then is it not just that she should return on those conditions, after she has published her defence in lyrical or any other metre? "

" Certainly."

" And we might also allow her champions, who are not poets, but lovers of poetry, to publish a prose defence on her behalf, showing that she is not only pleasant, but also useful for political constitutions and for human life, and we shall listen with friendly feelings. For it will be to our profit if she is made out to be not only pleasant, but useful."

" Most certainly to our profit," he said.

" But if not, my dear comrade, then, as men who have loved but have come to the conclusion that their love is unprofitable, though it may cost a struggle yet turn away; so likewise, though by reason of the love for such poetry that our nurture in beautiful constitutions has bred in us we shall be glad of any manifestation of her goodness and truth, yet until she is able to defend herself, we will not listen to her without repeating to ourselves as a charm this argument of ours and this incantation, for fear of falling again into that childish love which is still shared by the many. We shall chant, therefore, that this poetry is not to be taken seriously, as though it were a solemn performance which had to do with truth, but that he who hears it is to keep watch on it, fearful for the city in his soul, and that we must lay down these laws concerning poetry which we have described."

" I entirely agree with you," he said.

" For much is at stake, my dear Glaucon," I said, " more than people think, in a man's becoming good or bad; and therefore he must not be seduced by honour or money or any office, or even by poetry, to dare to neglect justice and the rest of virtue."

" What we have said makes me agree with you," he said; " and I think every one else would do the same."

A. D. LINDSAY.

Education and the Criterion of Art

LAWS 653–660.

Athenian Stranger. Let me once more recall our doctrine of right education; which, if I am not mistaken, depends on the due regulation of convivial intercourse.

Cleinias. You talk rather grandly.

Ath. Pleasure and pain I maintain to be the first perceptions of children, and I say that they are the forms under which virtue and vice are originally present to them.   As to wisdom and true and fixed opinions, happy is the man who acquires them, even when declining in years; and we may say that he who possesses them, and the blessings which are contained in them, is a perfect man.   Now I mean by education that training which is given by suitable habits to the first instincts of virtue in children;—when pleasure, and friendship, and pain, and hatred, are rightly implanted in souls not yet capable of understanding the nature of them, and who find them, after they have attained reason, to be in harmony with her.   This harmony of the soul, taken as a whole, is virtue; but the particular training in respect of pleasure and pain, which leads you always to hate what you ought to hate, and love what you ought to love from the beginning of life to the end, may be separated off; and, in my view, will be rightly called education.

Cle. I think, Stranger, that you are quite right in all that you have said and are saying about education.

Ath. I am glad to hear that you agree with me; for, indeed, the discipline of pleasure and pain which, when rightly ordered, is a principle of education, has been often relaxed and corrupted in human life. And the Gods, pitying the toils which our race is born to undergo, have appointed holy festivals, wherein men alternate rest with labour; and have given them the Muses and Apollo, the leader of the Muses, and Dionysus, to be companions in their revels, that they may improve their education by taking part in the festivals of the Gods, and with their help. I should like to know whether a common saying is in our opinion true to nature or not. For men say that the young of all creatures cannot be quiet in their bodies or in their voices; they are always wanting to move and cry out; some leaping and skipping, and overflowing with sportiveness and delight at something, others uttering all sorts of cries. But, whereas the animals have no perception of order or disorder in their movements, that is, of rhythm or harmony, as they are called, to us the Gods, who, as we say, have been appointed to be our companions in the dance, have given the pleasurable sense of harmony and rhythm; and so they stir us into life, and we follow them, joining hands together in dances and songs; and these they call choruses, which is a term naturally expressive of cheerfulness. Shall we begin, then, with the acknowledgment that education is first given through Apollo and the Muses? What do you say?

Cle. I assent.

Ath. And the uneducated is he who has not been trained in the chorus, and the educated is he who has been well trained?

Cle. Certainly.

Ath. And the chorus is made up of two parts, dance and song?

Cle. True.

Ath. Then he who is well educated will be able to sing and dance well?

Cle. I suppose that he will.

Ath. Let us see; what are we saying?

Cle. What?

Ath. He sings well and dances well; now must we add that he sings what is good and dances what is good?

Cle. Let us make the addition.

Ath. We will suppose that he knows the good to be good, and the bad to be bad, and makes use of them accordingly: which now is the better trained in dancing and music —he who is able to move his body and to use his voice in what is understood to be the right manner, but has no delight in good or hatred of evil; or he who is incorrect in gesture and voice, but is right in his sense of pleasure and pain, and welcomes what is good, and is offended at what is evil?

Cle. There is a great difference, Stranger, in the two kinds of education.

Ath. And if we three know what is good in song and dance, then we truly know also who is educated and who is uneducated; but if not, then we certainly shall not know wherein lies the safeguard of education, and whether there is any or not.

Cle. True.

Ath. Let us follow the scent like hounds, and go in pursuit of beauty of figure, and melody, and song, and dance; if these escape us, there will be no use in talking about true education, whether Hellenic or barbarian.

Cle. Yes.

Ath. And what is beauty of figure, or beautiful melody? When a manly soul is in trouble, and when a cowardly soul is in similar case, are they likely to use the same figures and gestures, or to give utterance to the same sounds?

Cle. How can they, when the very colours of their faces differ?

Ath. Good, my friend; I may observe, however, in passing, that in music there certainly are figures and there are melodies: and music is concerned with harmony and rhythm, so that you may speak of a melody or figure having good rhythm or good harmony—the term is correct enough; but to speak metaphorically of a melody or figure having a " good colour," as the masters of choruses do, is not allowable, although you can speak of the melodies or figures of the brave and the coward, praising the one and censuring the other.   And not to be tedious, let us say that the figures and melodies which are expressive of virtue of soul or body, or of images of virtue, are without exception good, and those which are expressive of vice are the reverse of good.

Cle. Your suggestion is excellent; and let us answer that these things are so.

Ath. Once more, are all of us equally delighted with every sort of dance?

Cle. Far otherwise.

Ath. What, then, leads us astray?   Are beautiful things not the same to us all, or are they the same in themselves, but not in our opinion of them?   For no one will admit that forms of vice in the dance are more beautiful than forms of virtue, or that he himself delights in the forms of vice, and others in a muse of another character.   And yet most persons say, that the excellence of music is to give pleasure to our souls.   But this is intolerable and blasphemous; there is, however, a much more plausible account of the delusion.

Cle. What?

Ath. The adaptation of art to the characters of men. Choric movements are imitations of manners occurring in various actions, fortunes, dispositions,—each particular is imitated, and those to whom the words, or songs, or dances are suited, either by nature or habit or both, cannot help feeling pleasure in them and applauding them, and calling them beautiful. But those whose natures, or ways, or habits are unsuited to them, cannot delight in them or applaud them, and they call them base. There are others, again, whose natures are right and their habits wrong, or whose habits are right and their natures wrong, and they praise one thing, but are pleased at another. For they say that all these imitations are pleasant, but not good. And in the presence of those whom they think wise, they are ashamed of dancing and singing in the baser manner, or of deliberately lending any countenance to such proceedings; and yet, they have a secret pleasure in them.

Cle. Very true.

Ath. And is any harm done to the lover of vicious dances or songs, or any good done to the approver of the opposite sort of pleasure?

Cle. I think that there is.

Ath. "I think" is not the word, but I would say, rather, "I am certain." For must they not have the same effect as when a man associates with bad characters, whom he likes and approves rather than dislikes, and only censures playfully because he has a suspicion of his own badness? In that case, he who takes pleasure in them will surely become like those in whom he takes pleasure, even though he be ashamed to praise them. And what greater good or evil can any destiny ever make us undergo?

Cle. I know of none.

Ath. Then in a city which has good laws, or in future ages is to have them, bearing in mind the instruction and amusement which are given by music, can we suppose that the poets are to be allowed to teach in the dance anything which they themselves like, in the way of rhythm, or melody, or words, to the young children of any well-conditioned parents? Is the poet to train his choruses as he pleases, without reference to virtue or vice?

Cle. That is surely quite unreasonable, and is not to be thought of.

Ath. And yet he may do this in almost any state with the exception of Egypt.

Cle. And what are the laws about music and dancing in Egypt?

Ath. You will wonder when I tell you: Long ago they appear to have recognised the very principle of which we are now speaking—that their young citizens must be habituated to forms and strains of virtue.   These they fixed, and exhibited the patterns of them in their temples; and no painter or artist is allowed to innovate upon them, or to leave the traditional forms and invent new ones.   To this day, no alteration is allowed either in these arts, or in music at all.   And you will find that their works of art are painted or moulded in the same forms which they had ten thousand years ago;—this is literally true and no exaggeration,—their ancient paintings and sculptures are not a whit better or worse than the work of to-day, but are made with just the same skill.

Cle. How extraordinary!

Ath. I should rather say, How statesmanlike, how worthy of a legislator!   I know that other things in Egypt are not so well.   But what I am telling you about music is true and deserving of consideration, because showing that a lawgiver may institute melodies which have a natural truth and correctness without any fear of failure.   To do this, however, must be the work of God, or of a divine person; in Egypt they have a tradition that their ancient chants which have been preserved for so many ages are the composition of the Goddess Isis.   And therefore, as I was saying, if a person can only find in any way the natural melodies, he may confidently embody them in a fixed and legal form.   For the love of novelty which arises out of pleasure in the new and weariness of the old, has not strength enough to corrupt the consecrated song and dance, under the plea that they have become antiquated. At any rate, they are far from being corrupted in Egypt.

Cle. Your arguments seem to prove your point.

Ath. May we not confidently say that the true use of music and of choral festivities is as follows: We rejoice when we think that we prosper, and again we think that we prosper when we rejoice?

Cle. Exactly.

Ath. And when rejoicing in our good fortune, we are unable to be still?

Cle. True.

Ath. Our young men break forth into dancing and singing and we who are their elders deem that we are fulfilling our part in life when we look on at them. Having lost our agility, we delight in their sports and merry-making, because we love to think of our former selves; and gladly institute contests for those who are able to awaken in us the memory of our youth.

Cle. Very true.

Ath. Is it altogether unmeaning to say, as the common people do about festivals, that he should be adjudged the wisest of men, and the winner of the palm, who gives us the greatest amount of pleasure and mirth? For on such occasions, and when mirth is the order of the day, ought not he to be honoured most, and, as I was saying, bear the palm, who gives most mirth to the greatest number? Now is this a true way of speaking or of acting?

Cle. Possibly.

Ath. But, my dear friend, let us distinguish between different cases, and not be hasty in forming a judgment. One way of considering the question will be to imagine a festival at which there are entertainments of all sorts, including gymnastic, musical, and equestrian contests: the citizens are assembled; prizes are offered, and proclamation is made that any one who likes may enter the lists, and that he is to bear the palm who gives the most pleasure to the spectators—there is to be no regulation about the manner how; but he who is most successful in giving pleasure is to be crowned victor, and deemed to be the pleasantest of the candidates. What is likely to be the result of such a proclamation?

Cle. In what respect?

Ath. There would be various exhibitions: one man, like Homer, will exhibit a rhapsody, another a performance on the lute; one will have a tragedy, and another a comedy. Nor would there be anything astonishing in some one imagining that he could gain the prize by exhibiting a puppet-show. Suppose these competitors to meet, and not these only, but innumerable others as well—can you tell me who ought to be the victor?

Cle. I do not see how any one can answer you, or pretend to know, unless he has heard with his own ears the several competitors; the question is absurd.

Ath. Well, then, if neither of you can answer, shall I answer this question which you deem so absurd?

Cle. By all means.

Ath. If very small children are to determine the question, they will decide for the puppet-show.

Cle. Of course.

Ath. The older children will be advocates of comedy; educated women and young men, and people in general, will favour tragedy.

Cle. Very likely.

Ath. And I believe that we old men would have the greatest pleasure in hearing a rhapsodist recite well the *Iliad* and *Odyssey*, or one of the Hesiodic poems, and would award the victory to him. But, who would really be the victor?—that is the question.

Cle. Yes.

Ath. Clearly you and I will have to declare that those whom we old men adjudge victors ought to win; for our ways are far and away better than any which at present exist anywhere in the world.

Cle. Certainly.

Ath. Thus far I too should agree with the many, that the excellence of music is to be measured by pleasure. But the pleasure must not be that of chance persons; the fairest music is that which delights the best and best educated, and especially that which delights the one man who is preeminent in virtue and education. And therefore the judges must be men of character, for they will require both wisdom and courage; the true judge must not draw his inspiration from the theatre, nor ought he to be unnerved by the clamour of the many and his own incapacity; nor again, knowing the truth, ought he through cowardice and unmanliness carelessly to deliver a lying judgment, with the very same lips which have just appealed to the Gods before he judged. He is sitting not as the disciple of the theatre, but, in his proper place, as their instructor, and he ought to be the enemy of all pandering to the pleasure of the spectators. The ancient and common custom of Hellas, which still prevails in Italy and Sicily, did certainly leave the judgment to the body of spectators, who determined the victor by show of hands. But this custom has been the destruction of the poets; for they are now in the habit of composing with a view to please the bad taste of their judges, and the result is that the spectators instruct themselves;—and also it has been the ruin of the theatre; they ought to be having characters put before them better than their own, and so receiving a higher pleasure, but now by their own act the opposite result follows. What inference is to be drawn from all this? Shall I tell you?

Cle. What?

Ath. The inference at which we arrive for the third or fourth time is, that education is the constraining and directing of youth towards that right reason which the law affirms, and which the experience of the eldest and best has agreed to be truly right.   In order, then, that the soul of the child may not be habituated to feel joy and sorrow in a manner at variance with the law, and those who obey the law, but may rather follow the law and rejoice and sorrow at the same things as the aged—in order, I say, to produce this effect, chants appear to have been invented, which really enchant, and are designed to implant that harmony of which we speak.   And because the mind of the child is incapable of enduring serious training, they are called plays and songs, and are performed in play; just as when men are sick and ailing in their bodies, their attendants give them wholesome diet in pleasant meats and drinks, but unwholesome diet in disagreeable things, in order that they may learn, as they ought, to like the one, and to dislike the other. And similarly the true legislator will persuade, and, if he cannot persuade, will compel the poet to express, as he ought, by fair and noble words, in his rhythms, the figures, and in his melodies, the music of temperate and brave and in every way good men.

B. JOWETT.

The Degeneration of Music

LAWS 700–701.

Ath. In the first place, let us speak of the laws about music,—that is to say, such music as then existed,—in order that we may trace the growth of the excess of freedom from

the beginning. Now music was early divided among us into
certain kinds and manners. One sort consisted of prayers
to the Gods, which were called hymns; and there was
another and opposite sort called lamentations, and another
termed paeans, and another, celebrating the birth of Dionysus, called, I believe, "dithyrambs." And they used the
actual word "laws," or νόμοι, for another kind of song;
and to this they added the term "citharoedic." All these
and others were duly distinguished, nor were the performers
allowed to confuse one style of music with another. And
the authority which determined and gave judgment, and
punished the disobedient, was not expressed in a hiss, nor
in the most unmusical shouts of the multitude, as in our
days, nor in applause and clapping of hands. But the
directors of public instruction insisted that the spectators
should listen in silence to the end; and boys and their tutors,
and the multitude in general, were kept quiet by a hint from
a stick. Such was the good order which the multitude were
willing to observe; they would never have dared to give
judgment by noisy cries. And then, as time went on, the
poets themselves introduced the reign of vulgar and lawless
innovation. They were men of genius, but they had no
perception of what is just and lawful in music; raging
like Bacchanals and possessed with inordinate delights—
mingling lamentations with hymns, and paeans with dithyrambs; imitating the sounds of the flute on the lyre, and
making one general confusion; ignorantly affirming that
music has no truth, and, whether good or bad, can only be
judged of rightly by the pleasure of the hearer. And by
composing such licentious works, and adding to them words
as licentious, they have inspired the multitude with lawlessness and boldness, and made them fancy that they can judge
for themselves about melody and song. And in this way the
theatres from being mute have become vocal, as though they

had understanding of good and bad in music and poetry; and instead of an aristocracy, an evil sort of theatrocracy has grown up. For if the democracy which judged had only consisted of educated persons, no fatal harm would have been done; but in music there first arose the universal conceit of omniscience and general lawlessness;—freedom came following afterwards, and men, fancying that they knew what they did not know, had no longer any fear, and the absence of fear begets shamelessness. For what is this shamelessness, which is so evil a thing, but the insolent refusal to regard the opinion of the better by reason of an over-daring sort of liberty?

B. Jowett.

The Danger of Musical Innovation

Laws 796–804.

Ath. Now we must say what has yet to be said about the gifts of the Muses and of Apollo: before, we fancied that we had said all, and that gymnastic alone remained; but now we see clearly what points have been omitted, and should be first proclaimed; of these, then, let us proceed to speak.

Cle. By all means.

Ath. Let me tell you once more—although you have heard me say the same before—that caution must be always exercised, both by the speaker and by the hearer, about anything that is very singular and unusual. For my tale is one which many a man would be afraid to tell, and yet I have a confidence which makes me go on.

Cle. What have you to say, Stranger?

Ath. I say that in states generally no one has observed that the plays of childhood have a great deal to do with the permanence or want of permanence in legislation. For when plays are ordered with a view to children having the same plays, and amusing themselves after the same manner and finding delight in the same playthings, the more solemn institutions of the state are allowed to remain undisturbed. Whereas if sports are disturbed, and innovations are made in them, and they constantly change, and the young never speak of their having the same likings, or the same established notions of good and bad taste, either in the bearing of their bodies or in their dress, but he who devises something new and out of the way in figures and colours and the like is held in special honour, we may truly say that no greater evil can happen in a state; for he who changes the sports is secretly changing the manners of the young, and making the old to be dishonoured among them and the new to be honoured. And I affirm that there is nothing which is a greater injury to all states than saying or thinking thus. Will you hear me tell how great I deem the evil to be?

Cle. You mean the evil of blaming antiquity in states?

Ath. Exactly.

Cle. If you are speaking of that, you will find in us hearers who are disposed to receive what you say not unfavourably but most favourably.

Ath. I should expect so.

Cle. Proceed.

Ath. Well, then, let us give all the greater heed to one another's words. The argument affirms that any change whatever except from evil is the most dangerous of all things; that is true in the case of the seasons and of the winds, in the management of our bodies and the habits of our minds—true of all things except, as I said before, of the bad. He who looks at the constitution of individuals accustomed to eat any sort of meat, or drink any drink, or to do any work which they can get, may see that they are at first disordered by them, but afterwards, as time goes on, their bodies grow adapted to them, and they learn to know and like variety, and have good health and enjoyment of life; and if ever afterwards they are confined again to a superior diet, at first they are troubled with disorders, and with difficulty become habituated to their new food. A similar principle we may imagine to hold good about the minds of men and the natures of their souls. For when they have been brought up in certain laws, which by some Divine Providence have remained unchanged during long ages, so that no one has any memory or tradition of their ever having been otherwise than they are, then every one is afraid and ashamed to change that which is established. The legislator must somehow find a way of implanting this reverence for antiquity, and I would propose the following way:—People are apt to fancy, as I was saying before, that when the plays of children are altered they are merely plays, not seeing that the most serious and detrimental consequences arise out of the change; and they readily comply with the child's wishes instead of deterring him, not considering that these children who make innovations in their games, when they grow up to be men, will be different from the last generation of children, and, being different, will desire a different sort of life, and under the influence of this desire will want other institutions and laws; and no one of them reflects that there will follow what I just now called the greatest of evils to states. Changes in bodily fashions are no such serious evils, but frequent changes in the praise and censure of manners are the greatest of evils, and require the utmost prevision.

Cle. To be sure.

Ath. And now do we still hold to our former assertion, that rhythms and music in general are imitations of good and evil characters in men? What say you?

Cle. That is the only doctrine which we can admit.

Ath. Must we not, then, try in every possible way to prevent our youth from even desiring to imitate new modes either in dance or song? nor must any one be allowed to offer them varieties of pleasures.

Cle. Most true.

Ath. Can any of us imagine a better mode of effecting this object than that of the Egyptians?

Cle. What is their method?

Ath. To consecrate every sort of dance or melody. First we should ordain festivals,—calculating for the year what they ought to be, and at what time, and in honour of what Gods, sons of Gods, and heroes they ought to be celebrated; and, in the next place, what hymns ought to be sung at the several sacrifices, and with what dances the particular festival is to be honoured. This has to be arranged at first by certain persons, and, when arranged, the whole assembly of the citizens are to offer sacrifices and libations to the Fates and all the other Gods, and to consecrate the several odes to Gods and heroes: and if any one offers any other hymns or dances to any one of the Gods, the priests and priestesses, acting in concert with the guardians of the law, shall with the sanction of religion and the law, exclude him, and he who is excluded, if he do not submit, shall be liable all his life long to have a suit of impiety brought against him by any one who likes.

Cle. Very good.

Ath. In the consideration of this subject, let us remember what is due to ourselves.

Cle. To what are you referring?

Ath. I mean that any young man, and much more any old one, when he sees or hears anything strange or unaccustomed, does not at once run to embrace the paradox, but he stands considering, like a person who is at a place where three paths meet, and does not very well know his way—he may be alone or he may be walking with others, and he will say to himself and them, "Which is the way?" and will not

K

move forward until he is satisfied that he is going right. And this is what we must do inthe present instance:— A strange discussion on the subject of law has arisen, which requires the utmost consideration, and we should not at our age be too ready to speak about such great matters, or be confident that we can say anything certain all in a moment.

Cle. Most true.

Ath. Then we will allow time for reflection, and decide when we have given the subject sufficient consideration. But that we may not be hindered from completing the natural arrangement of our laws, let us proceed to the conclusion of them in due order; for very possibly, if God will, the exposition of them, when completed, may throw light on our present perplexity.

Cle. Excellent, Stranger; let us do as you propose.

Ath. Let us then affirm the paradox that strains of music are our laws (νόμοι), and this latter being the name which the ancients gave to lyric songs, they probably would not have very much objected to our proposed application of the word.   Some one, either asleep or awake, must have had a dreamy suspicion of their nature.   And let our decree be as follows:—No one in singing or dancing shall offend against public and consecrated models, and the general fashion among the youth, any more than he would offend against any other law.   And he who observes this law shall be blameless; but he who is disobedient, as I was saying, shall be punished by the guardians of the laws, and by the priests and priestesses.   Suppose that we imagine this to be our law.

Cle. Very good.

Ath. Can any one who makes such laws escape ridicule? Let us see.   I think that our only safety will be in first framing certain models for composers.   One of these models shall

be as follows:—If when a sacrifice is going on, and the
victims are being burnt according to law,—if, I say, any
one who may be a son or brother, standing by another
at the altar and over the victims, horribly blasphemes, will
not his words inspire despondency and evil omens and
forebodings in the mind of his father and of his other
kinsmen?

Cle. Of course.

Ath. And this is just what takes place in almost all our
cities. A magistrate offers a public sacrifice, and there come
in not one but many choruses, who take up a position a
little way from the altar, and from time to time pour forth all
sorts of horrible blasphemies on the sacred rites, exciting the
souls of the audience with words and rhythms and melodies
most sorrowful to hear; and he who at the moment when
the city is offering sacrifice makes the citizens weep most,
carries away the palm of victory? Now, ought we not to
forbid such strains as these? And if ever our citizens
must hear such lamentations, then on some unblest and
inauspicious day let there be choruses of foreign and hired
minstrels, like those hirelings who accompany the departed at
funerals with barbarous Carian chants. That is the sort of
thing which will be appropriate if we have such strains at all;
and let the apparel of the singers be, not circlets and ornaments
of gold, but the reverse. Enough of all this. I will simply
ask once more whether we shall lay down as one of our
principles of song——

Cle. What?

Ath. That we should avoid every word of evil omen;
let that kind of song which is of good omen be heard everywhere and always in our state. I need hardly ask again,
but shall assume that you agree with me.

Cle. By all means; that law is approved by the suffrages
of us all.

Ath. But what shall be our next musical law or type? Ought not prayers to be offered up to the Gods when we sacrifice?

Cle. Certainly.

Ath. And our third law, if I am not mistaken, will be to the effect that our poets, understanding prayers to be requests which we make to the Gods, will take especial heed that they do not by mistake ask for evil instead of good. To make such a prayer would surely be too ridiculous.

Cle Very true.

Ath. Were we not a little while ago quite convinced that no silver or golden Plutus should dwell in our state?

Cle. To be sure.

Ath. And what has it been the object of our argument to show? Did we not imply that the poets are not always quite capable of knowing what is good or evil? And if one of them utters a mistaken prayer in song or words, he will make our citizens pray for the opposite of what is good in matters of the highest import; than which, as I was saying, there can be few greater mistakes. Shall we then propose as one of our laws and models relating to the Muses——

Cle. What?—will you explain the law more precisely?

Ath. Shall we make a law that the poet shall compose nothing contrary to the ideas of the lawful, or just, or beautiful, or good, which are allowed in the state? nor shall he be permitted to communicate his compositions to any private individuals, until he shall have shown them to the appointed judges and the guardians of the law, and they are satisfied with them. As to the persons whom we appoint to be our legislators about music and as to the director of education, these have been already indicated. Once more then, as I have asked more than once, shall this be our third law, and type, and model—What do you say?

Cle. Let it be so, by all means.

Ath. Then it will be proper to have hymns and praises of the Gods, intermingled with prayers; and after the Gods prayers and praises should be offered in like manner to demigods and heroes, suitable to their several characters.

Cle. Certainly.

Ath. In the next place there will be no objection to a law that citizens who are departed and have done good and energetic deeds, either with their souls or with their bodies, and have been obedient to the laws, should receive eulogies; this will be very fitting.

Cle. Quite true.

Ath. But to honour with hymns and panegyrics those who are still alive is not safe; a man should run his course, and make a fair ending, and then we will praise him; and let praise be given equally to women as well as men who have been distinguished in virtue. The order of songs and dances shall be as follows:—There are many ancient musical compositions and dances which are excellent, and from these the newly-founded city may freely select what is proper and suitable; and they shall choose judges of not less than fifty years of age, who shall make the selection, and any of the old poems which they deem sufficient they shall include; any that are deficient or altogether unsuitable, they shall either utterly throw aside, or examine and amend, taking into their counsel poets and musicians, and making use of their poetical genius; but explaining to them the wishes of the legislator in order that they may regulate dancing, music, and all choral strains, according to the mind of the judges; and not allowing them to indulge, except in some few matters, their individual pleasures and fancies. Now the irregular strain of music is always made ten thousand times better by attaining to law and order, and rejecting the honeyed Muse—

—not however that we mean wholly to exclude pleasure, which is the characteristic of all music.   And if a man be brought up from childhood to the age of discretion and maturity in the use of the orderly, and severe music, when he hears the opposite he detests it, and calls it illiberal; but if trained in the sweet and vulgar music, he deems the severer kind cold and displeasing.   So that, as I was saying before, while he who hears them gains no more pleasure from the one than from the other, the one has the advantage of making those who are trained in it better men, whereas the other makes them worse.

Cle. Very true.

Ath. Again, we must distinguish and determine on some general principle what songs are suitable to women, and what to men, and must assign to them their proper melodies and rhythms.   It is shocking for a whole harmony to be inharmonical, or for a rhythm to be unrhythmical, and this will happen when the melody is inappropriate to them.   And therefore the legislator must assign to these also their forms. Now both sexes have melodies and rhythms which of necessity belong to them; and those of women are clearly enough indicated by their natural difference.   The grand, and that which tends to courage, may be fairly called manly; but that which inclines to moderation and temperance may be declared both in law and in ordinary speech to be the more womanly quality.   This then, will be the general order of them.

Let us now speak of the manner of teaching and imparting them, and the persons to whom, and the time when, they are severally to be imparted.   As the shipwright first lays down the lines of the keel, and thus, as it were, draws the ship in outline, so do I seek to distinguish the patterns of life, and lay down their keels according to the nature of different men's souls; seeking truly to consider by what means, and in what ways, we may go through the voyage of life best. Now human affairs are hardly worth considering in earnest, and yet we must be in earnest about them,—a sad necessity constrains us. And having got thus far, there will be a fitness in our completing the matter, if we can only find some suitable method of doing so. But what do I mean? Some one may ask this very question, and quite rightly, too.

Cle. Certainly.

Ath. I say that about serious matters a man should be serious, and about a matter which is not serious he should not be serious; and that God is the natural and worthy object of our most serious and blessed endeavours, for man, as I said before, is made to be the plaything of God, and this, truly considered, is the best of him, wherefore also every man and woman should walk seriously, and pass life in the noblest of pastimes, and be of another mind from what they are at present.

Cle. In what respect?

Ath. At present they think that their serious pursuits should be for the sake of their sports, for they deem war a serious pursuit, which must be managed well for the sake of peace; but the truth is, that there neither is, nor has been, nor ever will be, either amusement or instruction in any degree worth speaking of in war, which is nevertheless deemed by us to be the most serious of our pursuits. And therefore, as we say, every one of us should live the life of peace as long and as well as he can. And what is the right way of living? Are we to live in sports always? If so, in what kind of sports? We ought to live sacrificing, and singing, and dancing, and then a man will be able to propitiate the Gods, and to defend himself against his enemies and conquer them in battle. The type of song or dance by which he will propitiate them has been described, and the paths along which he is to proceed have been cut for him. He will go forward in the spirit of the poet [1] :—

> Telemachus, some things thou wilt thyself find in thy heart, but other things God will suggest; for I deem that thou wast not born or brought up without the will of the Gods.

And this ought to be the view of our alumni; they ought to think that what has been said is enough for them, and that any other things their Genius and God will suggest to them —he will tell them to whom, and when, and to what Gods severally they are to sacrifice and perform dances, and how they may propitiate the deities, and live according to the appointment of nature; being for the most part puppets, but having some little share of reality.

Megillus. You have a low opinion of mankind, Stranger.

Ath. Nay, Megillus, be not amazed, but forgive me:—I was comparing them with the Gods; and under that feeling I spoke. Let us grant, if you wish, that the human race is not to be despised, but is worthy of some consideration.

B. JOWETT.

Choice of Music and Poetry for Educative Purposes

LAWS 810–813.

Ath. A fair time for a boy of ten years old to spend in letters is three years; the age of thirteen is the proper time for him to begin to handle the lyre, and he may continue at this for another three years, neither more nor less, and whether his father or himself like or dislike the study, he is not to be allowed to spend more or less time in learning music than the law allows. And let him who disobeys the law be deprived of those youthful honours of which we shall hereafter speak. Hear, however, first of all, what the young ought to learn in the early

<hr>

[1] Homer, *Odyss.* iii. 26 foll.

years of life, and what their instructors ought to teach them.
They ought to be occupied with their letters until they
are able to read and write; but the acquisition of perfect
beauty or quickness in writing, if nature has not stimulated
them to acquire these accomplishments in the given number
of years, they should let alone. And as to the learning
of compositions committed to writing which are not set to
the lyre, whether metrical or without rhythmical divisions,
compositions in prose, as they are termed, having no rhythm
or harmony—seeing how dangerous are the writings handed
down to us by many writers of this class—what will you do
with them, O most excellent guardians of the law? or how
can the lawgiver rightly direct you about them? I believe
that he will be in great difficulty.

Cle. What troubles you, Stranger? and why are you so
perplexed in your mind?

Ath. You naturally ask, Cleinias, and to you and Megillus,
who are my partners in the work of legislation, I
must state the more difficult as well as the easier parts
of the task.

Cle. To what do you refer in this instance?

Ath. I will tell you. There is a difficulty in opposing
many myriads of mouths.

Cle. Well, and have we not already opposed the popular
voice in many important enactments?

Ath. That is quite true; and you mean to imply that the
road which we are taking may be disagreeable to some but
is agreeable to as many others, or if not to as many, at any
rate to persons not inferior to the others, and in company
with them you bid me, at whatever risk, to proceed along
the path of legislation which has opened out of our present
discourse, and to be of good cheer, and not to faint.

Cle. Certainly.

Ath. And I do not faint; I say, indeed, that we have

a great many poets writing in hexameter, trimeter, and all sorts of measures—some who are serious, others who aim only at raising a laugh—and all mankind declare that the youth who are rightly educated should be brought up in them and saturated with them; some insist that they should be constantly hearing them read aloud, and always learning them, so as to get by heart entire poets; while others select choice passages and long speeches, and make compendiums of them, saying that these ought to be committed to memory, if a man is to be made good and wise by experience and learning of many things. And you want me now to tell them plainly in what they are right and in what they are wrong?

Cle. Yes, I do.

Ath. But how can I in one word rightly comprehend all of them? I am of opinion, and, if I am not mistaken, there is a general agreement, that every one of these poets has said many things well and many things the reverse of well; and if this be true, then do I affirm that much learning is dangerous to youth.

Cle. How would you advise the guardian of the law to act?

Ath. In what respect?

Cle. I mean to what pattern should he look as his guide in permitting the young to learn some things and forbidding them to learn others? Do not shrink from answering.

Ath. My good Cleinias, I rather think that I am fortunate.

Cle. How so?

Ath. I think that I am not wholly in want of a pattern, for when I consider the words which we have spoken from early dawn until now, and which, as I believe, have been inspired by Heaven, they appear to me to be quite like a poem. When I reflected upon all these words of ours, I naturally felt pleasure, for of all the discourses which I have ever learnt or heard, either in poetry or prose, this seemed to me to be the justest, and most suitable for young men to hear; I cannot imagine any better pattern than this which the guardian of the law who is also the director of education can have. He cannot do better than advise the teachers to teach the young these words and any which are of a like nature, if he should happen to find them, either in poetry or prose, or if he come across unwritten discourses akin to ours he should certainly preserve them, and commit them to writing. And, first of all, he shall constrain the teachers themselves to learn and approve them, and any of them who will not, shall not be employed by him, but those whom he finds agreeing in his judgment, he shall make use of and shall commit to them the instruction and education of youth. And here and on this wise let my fanciful tale about letters and teachers of letters come to an end.

Cle. I do not think, Stranger, that we have wandered out of the proposed limits of the argument; but whether we are right or not in our whole conception, I cannot be very certain.

Ath. The truth, Cleinias, may be expected to become clearer when, as we have often said, we arrive at the end of the whole discussion about laws.

Cle. Yes.

Ath. And now that we have done with the teacher of letters, the teacher of the lyre has to receive orders from us.

Cle. Certainly.

Ath. I think that we have only to recollect our previous discussions, and we shall be able to give suitable regulations touching all this part of instruction and education to the teachers of the lyre.

Cle. To what do you refer?

Ath. We were saying, if I remember rightly, that the sixty years old choristers of Dionysus were to be specially quick in their perceptions of rhythm and musical composition, that they might be able to distinguish good and bad imitation, that is to say, the imitation of the good or bad soul when under the influence of passion, rejecting the one and displaying the other in hymns and songs, charming the souls of youth, and inviting them to follow and attain virtue by the way of imitation.

Cle. Very true.

Ath. And with this view the teacher and the learner ought to use the sounds of the lyre, because its notes are pure, the player who teaches and his pupil rendering note for note in unison; but complexity, and variation of notes, when the strings give one sound and the poet or composer of the melody gives another,—also when they make concords and harmonies in which lesser and greater intervals, slow and quick, or high and low notes, are combined,—or, again, when they make complex variations of rhythms, which they adapt to the notes of the lyre,—all that sort of thing is not suited to those who have to acquire a speedy and useful knowledge of music in three years; for opposite principles are confusing, and create a difficulty in learning, and our young men should learn quickly, and their mere necessary acquirements are not few or trifling, as will be shown in due course. Let the director of education attend to the principles concerning music which we are laying down. As to the songs and words themselves which the masters of choruses are to teach and the character of them, they have been already described by us, and are the same which, when consecrated and adapted to the different festivals, we said were to benefit cities by affording them an innocent amusement.

B. JOWETT.

IV. ARISTOTLE

Poetry's Place among the Imitative Arts

POETICS cap. 1–3.

OUR subject being Poetry, I propose to speak not only of the art in general, but also of its species and their respective capacities; of the structure of plot required for a good poem; of the number and nature of the constituent parts of a poem; and likewise of any other matters in the same line of inquiry. Let us follow the natural order and begin with the primary facts.

Epic poetry and Tragedy, as also Comedy, Dithyrambic poetry, and most flute-playing and lyre-playing, are all, viewed as a whole, modes of imitation. But at the same time they differ from one another in three ways, either by a difference of kind in their means, or by differences in the objects, or in the manner of their imitations.

I. Just as form and colour are used as means by some, who (whether by art or constant practice) imitate and portray many things by their aid, and the voice is used by others; so also in the above-mentioned group of arts, the means with them as a whole are rhythm, language, and harmony —used, however, either singly or in certain combinations. A combination of rhythm and harmony alone is the means in flute-playing and lyre-playing, and any other arts there may be of the same description, e.g. imitative piping. Rhythm alone, without harmony, is the means in the dancer's imitations; for even he, by the rhythms of his attitudes, may represent men's characters, as well as what they do and suffer. There is further an art which imitates by language alone,

115

without harmony, in prose or in verse, and if in verse, either in some one or in a plurality of metres. This form of imitation is to this day without a name. We have no common name for a mime of Sophron or Xenarchus and a Socratic Conversation; and we should still be without one even if the imitation in the two instances were in trimeters or elegiacs or some other kind of verse—though it is the way with people to tack on " poet " to the name of a metre, and talk of elegiac-poets and epic-poets, thinking that they call them poets not by reason of the imitative nature of their work, but indiscriminately by reason of the metre they write in. Even if a theory of medicine or physical philosophy be put forth in a metrical form, it is usual to describe the writer in this way: Homer and Empedocles, however, have really nothing in common apart from their metre; so that, if the one is to be called a poet, the other should be termed a physicist rather than a poet. We should be in the same position also, if the imitation in these instances were in all the metres, like the *Centaur* (a rhapsody in a medley of all metres) of Chaeremon; and Chaeremon one has to recognise as a poet. So much, then, as to these arts. There are, lastly, certain other arts, which combine all the means enumerated, rhythm, melody, and verse, e.g. Dithyrambic and Nomic poetry, Tragedy and Comedy; with this difference, however, that the three kinds of means are in some of them all employed together, and in others brought in separately, one after the other. These elements of difference in the above arts I term the means of their imitation.

II. The objects the imitator represents are actions, with agents who are necessarily either good men or bad—the diversities of human character being nearly always derivative from this primary distinction, since the line between virtue and vice is one dividing the whole of mankind. It follows, therefore, that the agents represented must be either above our own level of goodness, or beneath it, or just such as we are; in the same way as, with the painters, the personages of Polygnotus are better than we are, those of Pauson worse, and those of Dionysius just like ourselves. It is clear that each of the above-mentioned arts will admit of these differences, and that it will become a separate art by representing objects with this point of difference. Even in dancing, flute-playing, and lyre-playing such diversities are possible; and they are also possible in the nameless art that uses language, prose or verse without harmony, as its means; Homer's personages, for instance, are better than we are; Cleophon's are on our own level; and those of Hegemon of Thasos, the first writer of parodies, and Nicochares, the author of the *Diliad*, are beneath it. The same is true of the Dithyramb and the Nome: the personages may be presented in them with the difference exemplified in the . . . of . . . and Argas, and in the Cyclopses of Timotheus and Philoxenus. This difference it is that distinguishes Tragedy and Comedy also; the one would make its personages worse, and the other better, than the men of the present day.

III. A third difference in these arts is in the manner in which each kind of object is represented. Given both the same means and the same kind of object for imitation, one may either (1) speak at one moment in narrative and at another in an assumed character, as Homer does; or (2) one may remain the same throughout, without any such change; or (3) the imitators may represent the whole story dramatically, as though they were actually doing the things described.

As we said at the beginning, therefore, the differences in the imitation of these arts come under three heads, their means, their objects, and their manner.

So that as an imitator Sophocles will be on one side akin to Homer, both portraying good men; and on another to Aristophanes, since both present their personages as acting and doing.

I. Bywater.

Origins of Poetry

Poetics cap. 4.

It is clear that the general origin of poetry was due to two causes, each of them part of human nature.   Imitation is natural to man from childhood, one of his advantages over the lower animals being this, that he is the most imitative creature in the world, and learns at first by imitation. And it is also natural for all to delight in works of imitation. The truth of this second point is shown by experience: though the objects themselves may be painful to see, we delight to view the most realistic representations of them in art, the forms for example of the lowest animals and of dead bodies.   The explanation is to be found in a further fact: to be learning something is the greatest of pleasures not only to the philosopher but also to the rest of mankind, however small their capacity for it; the reason of the delight in seeing the picture is that one is at the same time learning—gathering the meaning of things, e.g. that the man there is so-and-so; for if one has not seen the thing before, one's pleasure will not be in the picture as an imitation of it, but will be due to the execution or colouring or some similar cause. Imitation, then, being natural to us—as also the sense of harmony and rhythm, the metres being obviously species of rhythms—it was through their original aptitude, and by a series of improvements for the most part gradual on their first efforts, that they created poetry out of their improvisations.

Poetry, however, soon broke up into two kinds according to the differences of character in the individual poets; for the graver among them would represent noble actions, and those of noble personages; and the meaner sort the actions of the ignoble. The latter ⎽lass produced invectives at first, just as others did hymns and panegyrics. We know of no such poem by any of the pre-Homeric poets, though there were probably many such writers among them; instances, however, may be found from Homer downwards, e.g. his *Margites*, and the similar poems of others. In this poetry of invective its natural fitness brought an iambic metre into use; hence our present term " iambic," because it was the metre of their " iambs" or invectives against one another. The result was that the old poets became some of them writers of heroic and others of iambic verse. Homer's position, however, is peculiar: just as he was in the serious style the poet of poets, standing alone not only through the literary excellence, but also through the dramatic character of his imitations, so too he was the first to outline for us the general forms of Comedy by producing not a dramatic invective, but a dramatic picture of the Ridiculous; his *Margites* in fact stands in the same relation to our comedies as the *Iliad* and *Odyssey* to our tragedies. As soon, however, as Tragedy and Comedy appeared in the field, those naturally drawn to the one line of poetry became writers of comedies instead of iambs, and those naturally drawn to the other, writers of tragedies instead of epics, because these new modes of art were grander and of more esteem than the old.

I. BYWATER.

The Essential Nature of Comedy

POETICS cap. 5.

As for Comedy, it is (as has been observed) an imitation of men worse than the average; worse, however, not as regards any and every sort of fault, but only as regards one

L

particular kind, the Ridiculous, which is a species of the Ugly. The Ridiculous may be defined as a mistake or deformity not productive of pain or harm to others; the mask, for instance, that excites laughter, is something ugly and distorted without causing pain.

I. BYWATER.

Definition of Tragedy : its Parts

POETICS cap. 6–9.

Reserving hexameter poetry and Comedy for consideration hereafter, let us proceed now to the discussion of Tragedy; before doing so, however, we must gather up the definition resulting from what has been said. A tragedy, then, is the imitation of an action that is serious and also, as having magnitude, complete in itself; in language with pleasurable accessories, each kind brought in separately in the parts of the work; in a dramatic, not in a narrative form; with incidents arousing pity and fear, wherewith to accomplish its catharsis of such emotions. Here by "language with pleasurable accessories" I mean that with rhythm and harmony or song superadded; and by "the kinds separately" I mean that some portions are worked out with verse only, and others in turn with song.

I. As they act the stories, it follows that in the first place the Spectacle (or stage-appearance of the actors) must be some part of the whole; and in the second Melody and Diction, these two being the means of their imitation. Here by "Diction" I mean merely this, the composition of the verses; and by "Melody," what is too completely understood to require explanation. But further: the subject represented also is an action; and the action involves agents, who must necessarily have their distinctive qualities both of character and thought, since it is from these that we ascribe

certain qualities to their actions. There are in the natural
order of things, therefore, two causes, Character and Thought,
of their actions, and consequently of their success or failure
in their lives. Now the action (that which was done)
is represented in the play by the Fable or Plot. The Fable,
in our present sense of the term, is simply this, the combination of the incidents, or things done in the story; whereas
Character is what makes us ascribe certain moral qualities
to the agents; and Thought is shown in all they say when
proving a particular point or, it may be, enunciating a general
truth. There are six parts consequently of every tragedy,
as a whole, that is, of such or such quality, viz. a Fable or
Plot, Characters, Diction, Thought, Spectacle, and Melody;
two of them arising from the means, one from the manner,
and three from the objects of the dramatic imitation; and
there is nothing else besides these six. Of these, its formative
elements, then, not a few of the dramatists have made due
use, as every play, one may say, admits of Spectacle, Character,
Fable, Diction, Melody, and Thought.

II. The most important of the six is the combination
of the incidents of the story. Tragedy is essentially an
imitation not of persons but of action and life, of happiness
and misery. All human happiness or misery takes the form
of action; the end for which we live is a certain kind of
activity, not a quality. Character gives us qualities, but
it is in our actions—what we do—that we are happy or the
reverse. In a play accordingly they do not act in order to
portray the Characters; they include the Characters for
the sake of the action. So that it is the action in it, i.e.
its Fable or Plot, that is the end and purpose of the tragedy;
and the end is everywhere the chief thing. Besides this,
a tragedy is impossible without action, but there may be
one without character. The tragedies of most of the
moderns are characterless—a defect common among poets

of all kinds, and with its counterpart in painting in Zeuxis as compared with Polygnotus; for whereas the latter is strong in character, the work of Zeuxis is devoid of it.   And again: one may string together a series of characteristic speeches of the utmost finish as regards Diction and Thought, and yet fail to produce the true tragic effect; but one will have much better success with a tragedy which, however inferior in these respects, has a Plot, a combination of incidents, in it. And again: the most powerful elements of attraction in Tragedy, the Peripeties[1] and Discoveries, are parts of the Plot.   A further proof is in the fact that beginners succeed earlier with the Diction and Characters than with the construction of a story; and the same may be said of nearly all the early dramatists.   We maintain, therefore, that the first essential, the life, and soul, so to speak, of Tragedy is the Plot; and that the Characters come second—compare the parallel in painting, where the most beautiful colours laid on without order will not give one the same pleasure as a simple black-and-white sketch of a portrait.   We maintain that Tragedy is primarily an imitation of action, and that it is mainly for the sake of the action that it imitates the personal agents.   Third comes the element of Thought, i.e. the power of saying whatever can be said, or what is appropriate to the occasion.   This is what, in the speeches in Tragedy, falls under the arts of Politics and Rhetoric; for the older poets make their personages discourse like statesmen, and the moderns like rhetoricians.   One must not confuse it with Character.   Character in a play is that which reveals the moral purpose of the agents, i.e. the sort of thing they seek or avoid, where that is not obvious —hence there is no room for Character in a speech on a purely indifferent subject.   Thought, on the other hand, is shown in all they say when proving or disproving some

---

[1] Sudden reversals of fortune.

particular point, or enunciating some universal proposition. Fourth among the literary elements is the Diction of the personages, i.e. as before explained, the expression of their thoughts in words, which is practically the same thing with verse as with prose.   As for the two remaining parts, the Melody is the greatest of the pleasurable accessories of Tragedy.   The Spectacle, though an attraction, is the least artistic of all the parts, and has least to do with the art of poetry.   The tragic effect is quite possible without a public performance and actors; and besides, the getting-up of the Spectacle is more a matter for the costumier than the poet.

Having thus distinguished the parts, let us now consider the proper construction of the Fable or Plot, as that is at once the first and the most important thing in Tragedy. We have laid it down that a tragedy is an imitation of an action that is complete in itself, as a whole of some magnitude; for a whole may be of no magnitude to speak of.   Now a whole is that which has beginning, middle, and end.   A beginning is that which is not itself necessarily after anything else, and which has naturally something else after it; an end is that which is naturally after something itself, either as its necessary or usual consequent, and with nothing else after it; and a middle, that which is by nature after one thing and has also another after it.   A well-constructed Plot, therefore, cannot either begin or end at any point one likes; beginning and end in it must be of the forms just described. Again: to be beautiful, a living creature, and every whole made up of parts, must not only present a certain order in its arrangement of parts, but also be of a certain definite magnitude.   Beauty is a matter of size and order, and therefore impossible either (1) in a very minute creature, since our perception becomes indistinct as it approaches instantaneity; or (2) in a creature of vast size—one, say, 1,000 miles long — as in that case, instead of the object being seen all at once, the unity and wholeness of it is lost to the beholder. Just in the same way, then, as a beautiful whole made up of parts, or a beautiful living creature, must be of some size, a size to be taken in by the eye, so a story or Plot must be of some length, but of a length to be taken in by the memory. As for the limit of its length, so far as that is relative to public performances and spectators, it does not fall within the theory of poetry. If they had to perform a hundred tragedies, they would be timed by water-clocks, as they are said to have been at one period. The limit, however, set by the actual nature of the thing is this: the longer the story, consistently with its being comprehensible as a whole, the finer it is by reason of its magnitude. As a rough general formula, " a length which allows of the hero passing by a series of probable or necessary stages from misfortune to happiness, or from happiness to misfortune," may suffice as a limit for the magnitude of the story.

The Unity of a Plot does not consist, as some suppose, in its having one man as its subject. An infinity of things befall that one man, some of which it is impossible to reduce to unity; and in like manner there are many actions of one man which cannot be made to form one action. One sees, therefore, the mistake of all the poets who have written a *Heracleid*, a *Theseid*, or similar poems; they suppose that, because Heracles was one man, the story also of Heracles must be one story. Homer, however, evidently understood this point quite well, whether by art or instinct, just in the same way as he excels the rest in every other respect. In writing an *Odyssey*, he did not make the poem cover all that ever befell his hero—it befell him, for instance, to get wounded on Parnassus and also to feign madness at the time of the call to arms, but the two incidents had no probable or necessary connection with one another—instead of doing that, he took an action with a Unity of the kind we are describing as the subject of the *Odyssey*, as also of the *Iliad*. The truth is that, just as in the other imitative arts one imitation is always of one thing, so in poetry the story, as an imitation of action, must represent one action, a complete whole, with its several incidents so closely connected that the transposal or withdrawal of any one of them will disjoin and dislocate the whole. For that which makes no perceptible difference by its presence or absence is no real part of the whole.

From what we have said it will be seen that the poet's function is to describe, not the thing that has happened, but a kind of thing that might happen, i.e. what is possible as being probable or necessary. The distinction between historian and poet is not in the one writing prose and the other verse—you might put the work of Herodotus into verse, and it would still be a species of history; it consists really in this, that the one describes the thing that has been, and the other a kind of thing that might be. Hence poetry is something more philosophic and of graver import than history, since its statements are of the nature rather of universals, whereas those of history are singulars. By a universal statement I mean one as to what such or such a kind of man will probably or necessarily say or do—which is the aim of poetry, though it affixes proper names to the characters; by a singular statement, one as to what, say, Alcibiades did or had done to him. In Comedy this has become clear by this time; it is only when their plot is already made up of probable incidents that they give it a basis of proper names, choosing for the purpose any names that may occur to them, instead of writing like the old iambic poets about particular persons. In Tragedy, however, they still adhere to the historic names; and for this reason: what convinces is the possible; now whereas we are not yet sure as to the possibility of that which has not happened, that which has happened is manifestly possible, else it would not have come to pass.   Nevertheless even in Tragedy there are some plays with but one or two known names in them, the rest being inventions; and there are some without a single known name, e.g. Agathon's *Antheus*, in which both incidents and names are of the poet's invention; and it is no less delightful on that account.   So that one must not aim at a rigid adherence to the traditional stories on which tragedies are based.   It would be absurd, in fact, to do so, as even the known stories are only known to a few, though they are a delight none the less to all.

It is evident from the above that the poet must be more the poet of his stories or Plots than of his verses, inasmuch as he is a poet by virtue of the imitative element in his work, and it is actions that he imitates.   And if he should come to take a subject from actual history, he is none the less a poet for that; since some historic occurrences may very well be in the probable and possible order of things; and it is in that aspect of them that he is their poet.

Of simple Plots and actions the episodic are the worst. I call the Plot episodic when there is neither probability nor necessity in the sequence of its episodes.   Actions of this sort bad poets construct through their own fault, and good ones on account of the players.   His work being for public performance, a good poet often stretches out a Plot beyond its capabilities, and is thus obliged to twist the sequence of incident.

Tragedy, however, is an imitation not only of a complete action, but also of incidents arousing pity and fear.   Such incidents have the very greatest effect on the mind when they occur unexpectedly and at the same time in consequence of one another; there is more of the marvellous in them then than if they happened of themselves or by mere chance. Even matters of chance seem most marvellous if there is an appearance of design as it were in them; as for instance the statue of Mitys at Argos killed the author of Mitys' death by falling down on him when a looker-on at a public spectacle; for incidents like that we think to be not without a meaning. A Plot, therefore, of this sort is necessarily finer than others.

I. BYWATER.

Plot and Characters

POETICS cap. 13–15.

The next points after what we have said above will be these: (1) What is the poet to aim at, and what is he to avoid, in constructing his Plots? and (2) What are the conditions on which the tragic effect depends?

We assume that, for the finest form of Tragedy, the Plot must be not simple but complex; and further, that it must imitate actions arousing pity and fear, since that is the distinctive function of this kind of imitation. It follows, therefore, that there are three forms of Plot to be avoided. (1) A good man must not be seen passing from happiness to misery, or (2) a bad man from misery to happiness. The first situation is not fear-inspiring or piteous, but simply odious to us. The second is the most untragic that can be; it has no one of the requisites of Tragedy; it does not appeal either to the human feeling in us, or to our pity, or to our fears. Nor, on the other hand, should (3) an extremely bad man be seen falling from happiness into misery. Such a story may arouse the human feeling in us, but it will not move us to either pity or fear; pity is occasioned by unde-served misfortune, and fear by that of one like ourselves; so that there will be nothing either piteous or fear-inspiring in the situation. There remains, then, the intermediate kind of personage, a man not pre-eminently virtuous and just, whose misfortune, however, is brought upon him not by vice and depravity but by some error of judgment, of the number of those in the enjoyment of great reputation and prosperity; e.g. Oedipus, Thyestes, and the men of note of similar families. The perfect Plot, accordingly, must have a single, and not (as some tell us) a double issue; the change in the hero's fortunes must be not from misery to happiness, but on the contrary from happiness to misery; and the cause of it must lie not in any depravity, but in some great error on his part; the man himself being either such as we have described, or better, not worse, than that. Fact also confirms our theory. Though the poets began by accepting any tragic story that came to hand, in these days the finest tragedies are always on the story of some few houses, on that of Alcmeon, Oedipus, Orestes, Meleager, Thyestes, Telephus, or any others that may have been involved, as either agents or sufferers, in some deed of horror. The theoretically best tragedy, then, has a Plot of this description. The critics, therefore, are wrong who blame Euripides for taking this line in his tragedies, and giving many of them an unhappy ending. It is, as we have said, the right line to take. The best proof is this: on the stage, and in the public performances, such plays, properly worked out, are seen to be the most truly tragic; and Euripides, even if his execution be faulty in every other point, is seen to be nevertheless the most tragic certainly of the dramatists. After this comes the construction of Plot which some rank first, one with a double story (like the *Odyssey*) and an opposite issue for the good and the bad personages. It is ranked as first only through the weakness of the audiences; the poets merely follow their public, writing as its wishes dictate. But the pleasure here is not that of Tragedy. It belongs rather to Comedy, where the bitterest enemies in the piece (e.g. Orestes and Aegisthus) walk off good friends at the end, with no slaying of any one by any one.

The tragic fear and pity may be aroused by the Spectacle; but they may also be aroused by the very structure and incidents of the play—which is the better way and shows the better poet. The Plot in fact should be so framed that, even without seeing the things take place, he who simply hears the account of them shall be filled with horror and pity at the incidents; which is just the effect that the mere recital of the story in *Oedipus* would have on one. To produce this same effect by means of the Spectacle is less artistic, and requires extraneous aid. Those, however, who make use of the Spectacle to put before us that which is merely monstrous and not productive of fear, are wholly out of touch with Tragedy; not every kind of pleasure should be required of a tragedy, but only its own proper pleasure.

The tragic pleasure is that of pity and fear, and the poet has to produce it by a work of imitation; it is clear, therefore, that the causes should be included in the incidents of his story. Let us see, then, what kinds of incident strike one as horrible, or rather as piteous. In a deed of this description the parties must necessarily be either friends, or enemies, or indifferent to one another. Now when enemy does it on enemy, there is nothing to move us to pity either in his doing or in his meditating the deed, except so far as the actual pain of the sufferer is concerned; and the same is true when the parties are indifferent to one another. Whenever the tragic deed, however, is done within the family—when murder or the like is done or meditated by brother on brother, by son on father, by mother on son, or son on mother—these are the situations the poet should seek after. The traditional stories, accordingly, must be kept as they are, e.g. the murder of Clytaemnestra by

Orestes and of Eriphyle by Alcmeon. At the same time even with these there is something left to the poet himself; it is for him to devise the right way of treating them. Let us explain more clearly what we mean by " the right way." The deed of horror may be done by the doer knowingly and consciously, as in the old poets, and in Medea's murder of her children in Euripides. Or he may do it, but in ignorance of his relationship, and discover that afterwards, as does the Oedipus in Sophocles. Here the deed is outside the play; but it may be within it, like the act of the Alcmeon in Astydamas, or that of the Telegonus in *Ulysses Wounded*. A third possibility is for one meditating some deadly injury to another, in ignorance of his relationship, to make the discovery in time to draw back. These exhaust the possibilities, since the deed must necessarily be either done or not done, and either knowingly or unknowingly.

The worst situation is when the personage is with full knowledge on the point of doing the deed, and leaves it undone. It is odious and also (through the absence of suffering) untragic; hence it is that no one is made to act thus except in some few instances, e.g. Haemon and Creon in *Antigone*. Next after this comes the actual perpetration of the deed meditated. A better situation than that, however, is for the deed to be done in ignorance, and the relationship discovered afterwards, since there is nothing odious in it, and the Discovery will serve to astound us. But the best of all is the last; what we have in *Cresphontes*, for example, where Merope, on the point of slaying her son, recognises him in time ; in *Iphigenia*, where sister and brother are in a like position ; and in *Helle*, where the son recognises his mother, when on the point of giving her up to her enemy.

This will explain why our tragedies are restricted (as we said just now) to such a small number of families. It was accident rather than art that led the poets in quest of subjects to embody this kind of incident in their Plots. They are still obliged, accordingly, to have recourse to the families in which such horrors have occurred.

On the construction of the Plot, and the kind of Plot required for Tragedy, enough has now been said.

In the Characters there are four points to aim at. First and foremost, that they shall be good. There will be an element of character in the play, if (as has been observed) what a personage says or does reveals a certain moral purpose; and a good element of character, if the purpose so revealed is good. Such goodness is possible in every type of personage, even in a woman or a slave, though the one is perhaps an inferior, and the other wholly a worthless being. The second point is to make them appropriate. The Character before us may be, say, manly; but it is not appropriate in a female Character to be manly, or clever. The third is to make them like the reality, which is not the same as their being good and appropriate, in our sense of the term. The fourth is to make them consistent and the same throughout; even if inconsistency be part of the man before one for imitation as presenting that form of character, he should still be consistently inconsistent. We have an instance of baseness of character, not required for the story, in the Menelaus in *Orestes*; of the incongruous and unbefitting in the lamentation of Ulysses in *Scylla*, and in the speech of Melanippe; and of inconsistency in *Iphigenia at Aulis*, where Iphigenia the suppliant is utterly unlike the later Iphigenia. The right thing, however, is in the Characters just as in the incidents of the play to endeavour always after the necessary or the probable; so that when-ever such-and-such a personage says or does such-and-such a thing, it shall be the probable or necessary outcome of his character; and whenever this incident follows on that, it shall be either the necessary or the probable consequence of it. From this one sees (to digress for a moment) that the Dénouement also should arise out of the plot itself, and not depend on a stage-artifice, as in *Medea*, or in the story of the arrested departure of the Greeks in the *Iliad*. The artifice must be reserved for matters outside the play—for past events beyond human knowledge, or events yet to come, which require to be foretold or announced; since it is the privilege of the Gods to know everything. There should be nothing improbable among the actual incidents. If it be unavoidable, however, it should be outside the tragedy, like the improbability in the *Oedipus* of Sophocles. But to return to the Characters. As Tragedy is an imitation of personages better than the ordinary man, we in our way should follow the example of good portrait-painters, who reproduce the distinctive features of a man, and at the same time, without losing the likeness, make him handsomer than he is. The poet in like manner, in portraying men quick or slow to anger, or with similar infirmities of character, must know how to represent them as such, and at the same time as good men, as Agathon and Homer have represented Achilles.

All these rules one must keep in mind throughout, and further, those also for such points of stage-effect as directly depend on the art of the poet, since in these too one may often make mistakes. Enough, however, has been said on the subject in one of our published writings.

I. Bywater.

Hints for Plot-construction

Poetics cap. 17.

At the time when he is constructing his Plots, and engaged on the Diction in which they are worked out, the poet should remember (1) to put the actual scenes as far as possible before his eyes. In this way, seeing everything with the vividness of an eye-witness as it were, he will devise what is appropriate, and be least likely to overlook incongruities. This is shown by what was censured in Carcinus, the return of Amphiaraus from the sanctuary; it would have passed unnoticed, if it had not been actually seen by the audience; but on the stage his play failed, the incongruity of the incident offending the spectators. (2) As far as may be, too, the poet should even act his story with the very gestures of his personages. Given the same natural qualifications, he who feels the emotions to be described will be the most convincing; distress and anger, for instance, are portrayed most truthfully by one who is feeling them at the moment. Hence it is that poetry demands a man with special gift for it, or else one with a touch of madness in him; the former can easily assume the required mood, and the latter may be actually beside himself with emotion. (3) His story, again, whether already made or of his own making, he should first simplify and reduce to a universal form, before proceeding to lengthen it out by the insertion of episodes. The following will show how the universal element in *Iphigenia*, for instance, may be viewed: A certain maiden having been offered in sacrifice, and spirited away from her sacrificers into another land, where the custom was to sacrifice all strangers to the Goddess, she was made there the priestess of this rite. Long after that the brother of the priestess happened to come; the fact, however, of the oracle having for a certain reason bidden him go thither, and his object in going, are outside the Plot of the play. On his coming he was arrested, and about to be sacrificed, when he revealed who he was—either as Euripides puts it, or (as suggested by Polyidus) by the not improbable exclamation: "So I too am doomed to be sacrificed, as my sister was"; and the disclosure led to his salvation. This done, the next thing, after the proper names have been fixed as a basis for the story, is to work in episodes or accessory incidents. One must mind, however, that the episodes are appropriate, like the fit of madness in Orestes, which led to his arrest, and the purifying, which brought about his salvation. In plays, then, the episodes are short; in epic poetry they serve to lengthen out the poem. The argument of the *Odyssey* is not a long one. A certain man has been abroad many years; Poseidon is ever on the watch for him, and he is all alone. Matters at home too have come to this, that his substance is being wasted and his son's death plotted by suitors to his wife. Then he arrives there himself after his grievous sufferings; reveals himself, and falls on his enemies: and the end is his salvation and their death. This being all that is proper to the *Odyssey*, everything else in it is episode.

I. BYWATER.

Comparison between Epic and Tragedy

POETICS cap. 26.

The question may be raised whether the epic or the tragic is the higher form of imitation. It may be argued that if the less vulgar is the higher, and the less vulgar is always that which addresses the better public, an art addressing any and every one is of a very vulgar order. It is a belief that their public cannot see the meaning, unless they add something themselves, that causes the perpetual movements of the performers—bad flute-players, for instance, rolling about, if quoit-throwing is to be represented, and pulling at the conductor, if Scylla is the subject of the piece. Tragedy, then, is said to be an art of this order—to be in fact just what the later actors were in the eyes of their predecessors;

for Mynniscus used to call Callippides "the ape," because
he thought he so overacted his parts; and a similar view
was taken of Pindarus also. All Tragedy, however, is
said to stand to the Epic as the newer to the older school
of actors. The one, accordingly, is said to address a cultivated audience, which does not need the accompaniment of gesture; the other, an uncultivated one. If,
therefore, Tragedy is a vulgar art, it must clearly be
lower than the Epic.

The answer to this is twofold. In the first place, one
may urge (1) that the censure does not touch the art of the
dramatic poet, but only that of his interpreter; for it is
quite possible to overdo the gesturing even in an epic recital,
as did Sosistratus, and in a singing contest, as did Mnasitheus
of Opus. (2) That one should not condemn all movement,
unless one means to condemn even the dance, but only
that of ignoble people—which is the point of the criticism
passed on Callippides and in the present day on others, that
their women are not like gentlewomen. (3) That Tragedy
may produce its effect even without movement or action in
just the same way as Epic poetry; for from the mere reading
of a play its quality may be seen. So that, if it be superior
in all other respects, this element of inferiority is no
necessary part of it.

In the second place, one must remember (1) that Tragedy
has everything that the Epic has (even the epic metre being
admissible), together with a not inconsiderable addition in
the shape of the Music (a very real factor in the pleasure
of the drama) and the Spectacle. (2) That its reality of
presentation is felt in the play as read, as well as in the play
as acted. (3) That the tragic imitation requires less space
for the attainment of its end; which is a great advantage,
since the more concentrated effect is more pleasurable than
one with a large admixture of time to dilute it—consider

M

the *Oedipus* of Sophocles, for instance, and the effect of
expanding it into the number of lines of the *Iliad*.
(4) That there is less unity in the imitation of the epic poets,
as is proved by the fact that any one work of theirs supplies
matter for several tragedies; the result being that, if they
take what is really a single story, it seems curt when briefly
told, and thin and waterish when on the scale of length
usual with their verse.   In saying that there is less unity
in an epic, I mean an epic made up of a plurality of actions,
in the same way as the *Iliad* and *Odyssey* have many such
parts, each one of them in itself of some magnitude; yet
the structure of the two Homeric poems is as perfect as
can be, and the action in them is as nearly as possible one
action.   If, then, Tragedy is superior in these respects,
and also besides these, in its poetic effect (since the two forms
of poetry should give us, not any or every pleasure, but the
very special kind we have mentioned), it is clear that, as
attaining the poetic effect better than the Epic, it will be
the higher form of art.

I. Bywater.

Diction

RHETORIC III. i. 8–ii. 7.

The first improvement in style was naturally made by
the poets; for words are instruments of imitation, and the
voice is the most imitative of all our organs.   Thus the art
of recitation, the art of acting, and more besides were formed.
And, as the poets seemed to have won their present reputation, even when their thoughts were poor, by force of their
style, the first prose style was led to become poetical, like
that of Gorgias.   To this day, indeed, the mass of the
uneducated think that such persons are the finest talkers.
It is not so, however, the diction of prose and the diction of
poetry are distinct.   This appears from what is happening

now: the writers of tragedies are themselves modifying their style; and, just as they passed from tetrameter to iambic, because the iambic measure is, of all, the most like conversation, so they have discarded all those words which violate the ordinary idiom, but which the earlier writers used for ornament, and which to this day the writers of hexameters so use. It is absurd, then, to imitate those who have themselves dropped the fashion; and it becomes plain that we need not enter minutely into the whole question of style, but need discuss only that style of which we are speaking. The other style has been treated in the *Poetics*.

These points, then, may be taken as discussed. One virtue of Diction may be defined to be clearness. This appears from the fact that, if our language does not express our meaning, it will not do its work. Again, diction ought to be neither low nor too dignified, but suitable to the subject. (The diction of poetry could hardly be called " low," yet it is not suitable to prose.) Diction is made clear by nouns and verbs used in their proper sense; it is raised and adorned by words of the other classes mentioned in the *Poetics*.[1] Deviation from the ordinary idiom makes diction more impressive; for, as men are differently impressed by foreigners and by their fellow-citizens, so are they affected by styles. Hence we ought to give a foreign air to our language; for men admire what is far from them, and what is admired is pleasant. In the case of *metrical* composition there are many things which produce this effect, and which are in place *there*; for the things and persons concerned are more out of the common. In prose the opportunities are much fewer, the subject-matter being humbler. Even in poetry, if fine language were used by a slave, or by a very young man, or about mere trifles, it would be somewhat unbecoming; even in poetry there

[1] c. xxii.

is a sliding scale of propriety.   We must disguise our art, then, and seem to speak naturally, not artificially;   the natural is persuasive, the artificial is the reverse;   for men are prejudiced against it, as against an insidious design, just as they are suspicious of doctored wines.   The difference is the same as between the voice of Theodôros and that of other actors;   *his* voice seems to belong to the speaker,—*theirs*, to other men.   A successful illusion is wrought when the composer picks his words from the language of daily life;   this is what Euripides does, and first hinted the way to do.

Language is composed of nouns and verbs,—nouns being of the various classes which have been examined in the *Poetics*.[1]   Strange words, compound words, words coined for the occasion, should be used sparingly and rarely:—*where*, we will say by-and-by.[2]   The reason of this has been given already:—the effect is too odd to be fitting.   Accepted terms, proper terms, and metaphors, are alone available for the diction of prose.   This appears from the fact that all men confine themselves to these: all men in talking use metaphors, and the accepted or proper terms for things; so it is plain that, if the composer is skilful, the foreign air will be given, the art may be concealed, and he will be clear. And this, we saw, is the excellence of rhetorical language. Equivocal terms are the class of words most useful to the sophist, for it is with the help of these that he juggles; synonyms are most useful to the poet.   By synonyms in ordinary use I mean, for instance, " to go " and " to walk ": —these are at once accepted and synonymous terms.

R. C. JEBB.

[1] c. xxi.   [2] c. iii. and vii.

Sources of Frigidity

RHETORIC III. iii. 1–7.

Frigidities of style have four sources. First, compound words. Thus Lykophron [1] speaks of the "*many-faced* heaven," "the *high-peaked* earth";—and the "*narrow-channelled* shore." [2] Gorgias spoke of the "*beggar-poet* flatterer"; "forsworn or *ultra - veracious*." Alkidamas [3] has—"the soul filling with passion, and the face becoming *flame-hued*"; "he thought that their zeal would prove *doom-fraught*"; he describes "the persuasiveness of his speech" as "end-fulfilling"; and "the floor of the sea" as "dark-hued." All these phrases seem poetical, because they are composite.

This is one source of frigidity. Another is the use of strange words. Thus, with Lykophron, Xerxes is a "mammoth man," Skiron a "fell wight"; Alkidamas offers a "playful theme" to poetry, and speaks of the "distraughtness of a man's nature"—"whetted with the untempered anger of his thought."

A third cause is the use of lengthy, unsuitable or frequent epithets. In poetry it is fitting to say "*white* milk"; but in prose such epithets are either somewhat unsuitable, or, when too abundant, they betray the trick, and make it clear that this is poetry. It is right enough to use some epithets: they relieve the monotony, and give an air of distinction to our style; but we should aim at a mean, for

---

[1] The rhetorician and sophist. Several of the following phrases may have come from a panegyric on Theseus and other Athenian heroes.

[2] A reference either to the Hellespont, or to the narrow path running along the Scironian cliffs in Megara.

[3] Alkidamas, a rhetorician and sophist of the fourth century, who was a pupil of Gorgias.

too much art does more harm than utter carelessness: the latter is not good, but the other is positively bad.   This is why Alkidamas seems frigid; his epithets are not the mere seasoning but the actual meat, so thickly packed and overgrown and obtrusive are they.   It is not " sweat " but the " *damp* sweat "; not " to the Isthmian games " but " to the *solemn festival* of the Isthmian games."   It is not " the laws," but " those laws which are *the kings of the state* "; not " with a rush," but " with the *impulse rushing from his soul*."   He does not say " having taken to himself a school of the Muses," but " to *Nature's* school of the Muses "; he speaks of the solicitude of his soul as " *sullen-visaged* "; he says not, " the winner of favour," but " the winner of *multitudinous* favour."   Again—" *dispenser* of pleasure to the hearers ";   " he hid it (not among branches, but) among the branches *of the wood*."   " He veiled "—not his body, but—" the *shame* of his body."   He calls the soul's desire " *mirror-like* "—(this being a compound word, as well as an epithet, so that we get poetry); and, in the same way, the excess of his depravity as " *abnormal*."   Hence, by using poetic language, they make their style absurd and frigid owing to the impropriety,—and obscure, owing to the wordiness; for, when the speaker reiterates what is already understood, he overclouds and darkens the sense.   People generally use compound words, when there is no name for a thing, and when the compound is easy,—as " *pastime* "; but, if this is carried too far, it becomes distinctly poetical. Thus, compound words are most useful to writers of dithyrambs,—the dithyramb being sonorous;—rare words to epic poetry, since the rarity has grandeur and boldness; metaphor, to iambic verse,—iambic verse being, as we have said, the present metre of tragedy.

The fourth and last source of frigidity is metaphor. Metaphors, too, may be unsuitable, either from their absur-

dity (comic poets have their metaphors), or from an excess
of tragic grandeur:—they are obscure, when they are far-
fetched. Thus Gorgias spoke of events being " fresh, with
the blood in them still "; " you sowed this shameful seed,
and have reaped this evil harvest." This is too poetical.
Again, Alkidamas calls philosophy " a fort planted on the
domain of the laws," and the *Odyssey* " a fair mirror of human
life." He speaks of " offering no such playful theme
to poetry." All these phrases fail to be winning, for the
reasons just given. The address of Gorgias to the swallow,
which had polluted his head in its flight, is a masterpiece
of the tragic style. " Nay," he said, " this is unseemly,
Philomêla." The act would not have been unbecoming in
a bird, but was unbecoming in a girl. It was a judicious
reproach, then, to call her what she was, and not what
she *is*.

R. C. JEBB.

The Different Styles of Rhetoric

RHETORIC III. xii. 1–6.

It must not be forgotten that each branch of Rhetoric
has its fitting style. There is a difference between the
literary and the agonistic style; and, in the latter, between
the parliamentary and the forensic style. It is necessary to
know both styles. A knowledge of the agonistic style
means simply the power of speaking good Greek; a knowledge of the literary style means not being tongue-tied,
when one wants to impart something to the world at large,
which is the case with those who have no skill in composition.
The literary style is the most accurate; the agonistic is the
best adapted to delivery. This fitness depends upon one
of two things: expression of character, or expression of
emotion. Hence actors seek plays, and poets personages,

of these types. The poets who write to be read have a circulation, however,—as Chaerêmôn,[1]—who has all the finish of a professional speech-writer—and among dithyrambic poets, Likymnios. On a comparison, the speeches of the literary men seem thin in actual contests, while speeches by orators, which were well delivered, seem unworkmanlike when they are read. The reason is that their style is suitable only in the arena of debate. For the same reason, devices suited to delivery, when not helped by delivery, seem silly because they are not doing their proper work. Thus *asyndeta* and reiterations of the same word are rightly reprobated in the literary style, but not so in the agonistic style,—indeed public speakers use them, for they are dramatic. But when we reiterate, we must also vary,—an art which is, as it were, introductory to the whole art of delivery. " *This* is the thief in your midst —*this* is the knave—*this* is he who finally sought to be a traitor." Philêmôn, the actor, illustrated this by his delivery of the passage about Rhadamanthys and Palamêdês in the *Gerontomania* of Anaxandrides, and by his pronunciation of " I " in the prologue to the " Good Men ": indeed, if one is not dramatic in such repetitions, it becomes a case of " the man who carries the beam." So it is, too, with *asyndeta*. " I came—I met him—I made my petition ": one must *act* this,—not say it as if it was a single clause, with unvarying sentiment and tone. *Asyndeta* have this further property—a greater number of things seems to have been said in an equal time; for it is the connecting particle which makes one of many, and so, if the connecting particle is removed, of course many will be made out of one. Hence *Asyndeton* serves to amplify:—" I came, I spoke to him, I

---

[1] The tragic poet already quoted in *Rhet*. II. xxiii. 29. His elaborate finish is exemplified by his enumeration of all the flowers in a garland, *Athen*. 679 F.

besought " (these seem *many* things); " he disregarded all that I said." This is what Homer[1] wishes to do in the passage:—

> Nireus, again, from Symê—
> Nireus, son of Aglaia—
> Nireus, fairest of all—.

A person of whom *much* is said must needs be mentioned *often*; if, then, he is mentioned *often*, it seems as if *much* were said; a fallacy which has enabled the poet to make Nireus important by a single mention, though nowhere does he say a word about him afterwards.

The Deliberative style, then, is exactly like rough fresco-painting :—the larger the audience, the more distant the spectacle;—in both, then, minute touches are superfluous, and are seen at a disadvantage. The Forensic style is more finished; most so, when the cause is heard by a single judge ; for then it depends least upon rhetorical artifices ; the relevant and the irrelevant are then more easily seen in one view, and the turmoil is absent, so that the judgment is serene. Hence the same speakers are not brilliant in all these different kinds; where there is most room for declamation, there finish is least in place; and this is where voice, especially loudness of voice, has scope.

The Epideiktic style is the best suited to writing; for it is doing its own work when it is being read;— next, the Forensic.

A further classification of style, according to its need to be " sweet " or "magnificent," is unnecessary. Why these, rather than " temperate," " liberal," or any other note of moral virtue ? " Sweet," of course, it will be made by the qualities above mentioned,—assuming the excellence of style to have been rightly defined. With what other object is it to be " clear," and " not grovelling," but " suited

---

[1] *Iliad* ii. 671 f.

to the subject " ?   If it is diffuse, or if, again, it is curt, it will not be " clear ": the fitting thing is plainly the mean.   Sweetness will be given to style by the happy mixture of the things aforesaid—the familiar and the foreign, and the rhythm, and that persuasiveness which comes of propriety.

R. C. JEBB.

V. DIONYSIUS OF HALICARNASSUS

The Three Styles of Composition

De Compositione Verborum cap. xxi.–xxiv.

I ASSERT without any hesitation that there are many specific differences of composition, and that they cannot be brought into a comprehensive view or within a precise enumeration; I think too that, as in personal appearance, so also in literary composition, each of us has an individual character. I find not a bad illustration in painting. As in that art all painters from life take the same pigments but mix them in the most diverse ways, so in poetry and in prose, though we all use the same words, we do not put them together in the same manner. I hold, however, that the essentially different varieties of composition are the three following only, to which any one who likes may assign the appropriate names, when he has heard their characteristics and their differences. For my own part, since I cannot find recognised names for them, inasmuch as none exist, I call them by metaphorical terms—the first *austere*, the second *smooth* (or *florid*), the third *harmoniously blended*. How I am to say the third is formed I am at a loss to know—" my mind is too divided to utter truth " : [1] I cannot see whether it is formed by eliminating the two extremes or by fusing them—it is not easy to hit on any clear answer. Perhaps, then, it is better to say that it is by relaxation and tension of the extremes that the means, which are very numerous, arise. The case is not as in music, where the middle note is equally removed from the lowest and the highest. The middle

[1] Pindar, *Fragm.* 213 (Schroeder).

145

style in writing does not in the same way stand at an equal distance from each of the two extremes; "middle" is here a vague general term, like "herd," "heap," and many others. But the present is not the right time for the investigation of this particular point. I must say what I undertook to say with regard to the several styles—not all that I could (I should need a very long treatise to do that), but just the most salient points.

The characteristic feature of the austere arrangement is this:—It requires that the words should be like columns firmly planted and placed in strong positions, so that each word should be seen on every side, and that the parts should be at appreciable distances from one another, being separated by perceptible intervals. It does not in the least shrink from using frequently harsh sound-clashings which jar on the ear; like blocks of building stone that are laid together unworked, blocks that are not square and smooth, but preserve their natural roughness and irregularity. It is prone for the most part to expansion by means of great spacious words. It objects to being confined to short syllables, except under occasional stress of necessity.

In respect of the words, then, these are the aims which it strives to attain, and to these it adheres. In its clauses it pursues not only these objects but also impressive and stately rhythms, and tries to make its clauses not parallel in structure or sound, nor slaves to a rigid sequence, but noble, brilliant, free. It wishes them to suggest nature rather than art, and to stir emotion rather than to reflect character. And as to periods, it does not, as a rule, even attempt to compose them in such a way that the sense of each is complete in itself: if it ever drifts into this accidentally, it seeks to emphasise its own unstudied and simple character, neither using any supplementary words which in no way aid the sense, merely in order that the period may be fully rounded off, nor being anxious that the periods should move smoothly or showily, nor nicely calculating them so as to be just sufficient (if you please) for the speaker's breath, nor taking pains about any other such trifles. Further, the arrangement in question is marked by flexibility in its use of the cases, variety in the employment of figures, few connectives; it lacks articles, it often disregards natural sequence; it is anything rather than florid, it is aristocratic, plain-spoken, unvarnished; an old-world mellowness constitutes its beauty.

This mode of composition was once zealously practised by many authors in poetry, history, and civil oratory; pre-eminently in epic poetry by Antimachus of Colophon and Empedocles the natural philosopher, in lyric poetry by Pindar, in tragedy by Aeschylus, in history by Thucydides, and in civil oratory by Antiphon. At this point the subject would naturally call for the presentation of numerous examples of each author cited, and possibly the discourse would have been rendered not unattractive if bedecked with many such flowers of spring. But then the treatise would probably be felt to be excessively long—more like a course of lectures than a manual. On the other hand, it would not be fitting to leave the statements unsubstantiated, as though they were obvious and not in need of proof. The right thing, no doubt, is after all to take a sort of middle course, neither to exceed all measure, nor yet to fall short of carrying conviction. I will endeavour to do so by selecting a few samples from the most distinguished authors. Among poets it will be enough to cite Pindar, among prose-writers Thucydides; for these are the best writers in the austere style of composition. . . .

The smooth (or florid) mode of composition, which I regarded as second in order, has the following features. It does not intend that each word should be seen on every side, nor that all its parts should stand on broad, firm bases, nor that the time-intervals between them should be long; nor in general is this slow and deliberate movement congenial to it. It demands free movement in its diction; it requires words to come sweeping along one on top of another, each supported by that which follows, like the onflow of a never-resting stream. It tries to combine and interweave its component parts, and thus give, as far as possible, the effect of one continuous utterance. This result is produced by so nicely adjusting the junctures that they admit no appreciable time-interval between the words. From this point of view the style resembles finely woven stuffs, or pictures in which the lights melt insensibly into the shadows. It requires that all its words shall be melodious, smooth, soft, as a maiden's face; and it shrinks from harsh, clashing syllables, and carefully avoids everything rash and hazardous.

It requires not only that its words should be properly dovetailed and fitted together, but also that the clauses should be carefully inwoven with one another and all issue in a period. It limits the length of a clause so that it is neither shorter nor longer than the right mean, and the compass of the period so that a man's full breath will be able to cover it. It could not endure to construct a passage without periods, nor a period without clauses, nor a clause without symmetry. The rhythms it uses are not the longest, but the intermediate, or shorter than these. It requires its periods to march as with steps regulated by line and rule, and to close with a rhythmical fall. Thus, in fitting together its periods and its words respectively, it employs two different methods. The latter it runs together; the former it keeps apart, wishing that they may be seen as it were from every side. As for figures, it is wont to employ not the most time-honoured sort, nor those marked by state-liness, gravity, or mellowness, but rather for the most part those which are dainty and alluring, and contain much that is seductive and fanciful. To speak generally: its attitude is directly opposed to that of the former variety in the principal and most essential points. I need not go over these points again.

Our next step will be to enumerate those who have attained eminence in this style. Well, among epic poets Hesiod, I think, has best developed the type; among lyric poets, Sappho, and, after her, Anacreon and Simonides; of tragedians, Euripides alone; of historians, none exactly, but Ephorus and Theopompus more than most; of orators, Isocrates. I will quote examples of this style also, selecting among poets Sappho, and among orators Isocrates.

The third kind of composition is the mean between the two already mentioned. I call it *harmoniously blended* for lack of a proper and better name. It has no form peculiar to itself, but is a sort of judicious blend of the two others and a selection from the most effective features of each. This kind, it seems to me, deserves to win the first prize; for it is a sort of mean, and excellence in life and conduct and the arts is a mean, according to Aristotle and the other philosophers of his school. As I said before, it is to be viewed not narrowly but broadly. It has many specific varieties. Those who have adopted it have not all had the same aims nor the same methods; some have made more use of this method, others of that; while the same methods have been pursued with less or greater vigour by different writers, who have yet all achieved eminence in the various walks of literature. Now he who towers conspicuous above them all,

> Out of whose fulness all rivers, and every sea, have birth,
> And all upleaping fountains,[1]

is, we must admit, Homer. For whatever passage you like

[1] Homer, *Iliad* xxi. 196–197.

to take in him has had its manifold charms brought to perfection by a union of the severe and the polished forms of arrangement.   Of the other writers who have cultivated the same golden mean, all will be found to be far inferior to Homer when measured by his standard, but still men of eminence when regarded in themselves: among lyric poets Stesichorus and Alcaeus, among tragedians Sophocles, among historians Herodotus, among orators Demosthenes, and among philosophers (in my opinion) Democritus, Plato, and Aristotle.   It is impossible to find authors who have succeeded better in blending their writings into harmonious wholes.   As regards types of composition the foregoing remarks will suffice.   I do not think it necessary to quote specimen passages from the authors just mentioned, since they are known to all and need no illustration.

W. Rhys Roberts.

The Decline and Revival of Greek Oratory

De Antiquis Oratoribus §§ 1–4.

We ought to feel very grateful to the times we live in, my dear Ammaeus, for improvement in many studies, and most particularly for the great advance made in political oratory.   In the epoch before ours, the old philosophic type of Rhetoric, subjected to monstrous ill-treatment, was being destroyed.   From the death of Alexander of Macedon she had gradually withered and declined, till in our own day she was almost gone.   A new type of Rhetoric had supplanted her, an ill-bred, pretentious Rhetoric of intolerable effrontery, devoid of philosophy and every form of liberal education.   Undetected by the ignorant and deluded mob, this new Rhetoric not only lived in greater wealth and luxury and magnificence than the other, but had actually attached to herself the posts of honour and political importance

which should have belonged to her philosophic sister. She
was a thoroughly vulgar and disagreeable person, and finally
she made Greece resemble the house of a miserable debauchee.
Just as in such a house the free-born, respectable wife sits
deprived of all power over her possessions, while a giddy
lady of pleasure, who is there to ruin the property, claims to
rule the whole establishment, terrorising the other and
treating her like dirt: so it happened in every city in Greece,
and, to crown all, in the educated ones as much as any.
The ancient, indigenous Muse of Athens was reduced to a
position of insignificance, expelled from her own possessions,
while her rival, a parvenue from some Asiatic jail, some
Phrygian or Carian or barbarian creature, claimed to
administer Hellenic cities, driving the other out of public
life. Thus the ignoramus expelled the philosopher, the
mad the sane.

However, it is not only of just men that, as Pindar says:
" time is the surest saviour," but of arts and studies and all
else that is good. Our own day has proved that. Whether the
initiative came from some god, or from nature's cycle bringing round the ancient order again, or from an impulse in mankind urging many people in the same direction: whichever it
was, the present age has restored to the ancient, sober Rhetoric
her former merited repute, and has compelled the new, silly
Rhetoric to cease enjoying the fruits of a distinction to which
she has no claim, and living luxuriously on the good things
of another. Nor perhaps should we merely commend the
present age, and the philosophers who aided it, for initiating
a betterment of taste (though it is truly said that the beginning
is half the whole), but also for effecting so swift a revolution
and so striking an improvement. There are a few cities
in Asia whose ignorance makes them slow to learn
what is noble. But the rest of the world has stopped
admiring vulgar, frigid and stupid oratory. Those who

N

formerly prided themselves on such productions are learning shame, and are gradually deserting to the other side, except for a few incurables: while those who are just beginning their studies bring these speeches into contempt, and ridicule the idea of taking them seriously.

I think that the cause and origin of this great revolution was the universal supremacy of Rome, which compelled all other cities to look to her for a lead: and, in Rome itself, the high degree of education and the fine critical faculty attained by a governing class which ruled the state in virtue of merit, and in accordance with the highest principles. Under its discipline the sensible element in the state has further increased, and the foolish element has been compelled to be reasonable. That is why so many excellent histories are written nowadays, and so many interesting political treatises are published, not to mention by no means contemptible works on philosophy. Many other admirable subjects, which both Romans and Greeks have enthusiastically studied, have advanced considerably and will in all probability advance still further. After seeing so great a revolution take place in this short time, I should not be astonished if this taste for silly speeches lasted no longer than one more generation. When something that formerly filled the world has shrunk to a narrow compass, it is easy for it to vanish altogether.

But enough of returning thanks to Time for the change he is bringing about, of praising those who choose the better path, of conjecturing the future from the past, and so forth. These are things that any one could do. I will now try to explain how the good cause can be still further reinforced. I will take as my subject an enquiry of general interest and of great advantage to humanity. Who are the most note-worthy of the ancient orators and historians? What principles did they follow in life and literature? What ought we to derive from each of them and what ought we to avoid ? These are noble subjects for investigation and necessary to all students of political philosophy, yet they are not hackneyed or exhausted by previous writers. Personally, at any rate, I do not remember ever having met with such a treatise, although I searched diligently enough. I make no definite assertion, nor do I pretend to accurate knowledge. There may be writings of the kind which have escaped me. It is arbitrary to the point of madness for a man to constitute himself the authority on all points of learning, and declare that something has never happened which might well have happened. Very well then, as I say, I can make no positive assertion on this point. Now the orators and historians with whom I am concerned (taking the good ones only) are numerous, and to deal with them all would, I realise, be a long business. So I shall not attempt this, but instead shall select the most attractive from the different epochs, and describe each in turn. For the present I shall occupy myself with the orators. Subsequently, if I have the opportunity, I shall also treat the historians. I shall select three orators of the older school, Lysias, Isocrates and Isaeus, and three from their successors, Demosthenes, Hyperides and Aeschines. These six I consider the greatest. My treatise will be divided into two parts. It will begin with an account of the older orators. After this preface, it is time to return to my subject.

The Style of Isocrates

DE ISOCRATE § 2.

His style may be summed up as follows : It is as pure as Lysias', and not a word is used at random. His language is the perfection of normal everyday Greek. Like Lysias, he avoids the tasteless use of obsolete and peculiar terms, though he differs from him slightly in his employment of figurative language. Isocrates' manner is happily blended. In clearness and vividness he runs Lysias close. His style is expressive of character, persuasive and appropriate. It has not, however, the rounded compactness which makes Lysias so suitable for the law-courts. Rather it sprawls in a certain rich profusion. It is not so concise: its gait is ungainly and excessively deliberate. I shall explain why in a moment. Its arrangement is not, like that of Lysias, natural, simple and vigorous, but artificially stately, ceremonious and elaborate: in one way more striking than Lysias, in another more finicky. Here is a man who seeks beauty of expression by every means, and aims at polish rather than simplicity. He avoids the juxtaposition of vowels, as breaking the melodic flow and spoiling the smoothness of the sound. He attempts to embrace his ideas within the circle of a strongly rhythmic period, which is not far removed from poetical metre. He is better for reading than for practical use. That is why his speeches stand the test of recitation at a festival or of reading in private, but fail in the battles of the assembly or law-court. The reason is that the latter occasions demand a great deal of emotion: and emotion is the last thing that the periodic style admits. Similarity of cadence, balance of clauses, antithesis, the whole apparatus of such figures, are freely found in him, and often spoil his work by offending the ear.

Criticism of Isocrates

DE DEMOSTHENE § 18.

Such is the style of Isocrates, which is considered the finest of all. It is in many respects worthy of admiration. No style is purer in diction, more precise in idiom. It is straightforward and normal. It possesses all the other chief merits which can make style lucid. It has also many of the accessory [1] adornments. It is lofty, stately, dignified, beautiful as regards vocabulary, pleasing, and reasonably graceful. But it is not perfect in this respect. It may be censured as deficient in some important points. First of all, in conciseness: aiming at clearness, it often neglects moderation, whereas it should have provided for both. Secondly, in compactness. It is floppy and spun-out, and its sentences overflow, like those of the historians. But the style of active debate wants to be rounded and hammered, with no bulging protuberances. Again, there are other defects in Isocrates. He is timid in his use of metaphor, shies at noise, and never introduces a note of intensity. Yet wrestlers in the arena of life must have a firm touch and a relentless grip. He cannot stir the emotions of an audience as much as he wishes: and for the most part he does not wish. He is convinced that it is enough for a politician to manifest good intentions and a respectable character. And, to give him his due, he does succeed in doing that. But after all, the most potent resource for a man who wants to persuade a public assembly or a jury is to arouse the emotions of his audience.

Again, Isocrates does not always hit off what the moment requires. Sometimes he misses it, demanding, as he does, that language should be flowery and effective at all costs, on the view that in literature pleasure is supreme. In reality, all subjects do not demand the same manner of expression. Just as there are clothes which suit particular human bodies, so there is language which suits particular thoughts. To sweeten sound by any and every means, selecting suave and euphonious words, to consider it necessary to embrace

---

[1] In *De Thucydide*, 23, Dionysius enumerates the "necessary" virtues of style: "purity," "lucidity" and "conciseness." All other virtues are "accessory."

everything in rhythmically compacted periods, and to beautify a speech by showy figures, is not always advantageous. That is a lesson we can learn from the great writers of epic, tragic and lyric poetry, who cared less for giving pleasure than for truth.

Comparison between Lysias and Isocrates

DE ISOCRATE § 12.

So much for the style of the two. When I turned to examine their treatment of subject-matter, I found that each showed amazing inventiveness and discrimination. But in the marshalling of points, the ordering of arguments and the working out of both, in fact, in the whole domain of subject-matter, I considered Isocrates far ahead of Lysias; while in respect of the splendour of his themes, and the philosophic nature of his purpose, I found him as superior to Lysias as a grown man to a child, as Plato said: superior, in fact, if truth be told, to all other orators who worked at oratory in a philosophic spirit. But I could not approve the rounded construction of his periods, or the affectation of his turns of phrase. Often the thought is the slave of the rhythm and realism is sacrificed to prettiness. In the strenuous language of politics, the best method is the nearest to nature. And nature demands that the style should follow the thought, not the thought the style. When a statesman is talking about war and peace, or a private individual is fighting for his life before a jury, I do not see what can be the good of these theatrical refinements and affectations. Or rather, I know that they are likely to be prejudicial. All prettiness, employed at a serious moment and in time of trouble, is unseasonable and alienates sympathy.

Comparison between Lysias *and* Demosthenes

DE DEMOSTHENE § 13.

What then is the difference between the two even here ? And how can one distinguish, when Demosthenes cuts himself down to bare necessities, his superiority over Lysias in style alone ? You want to know this as well. As I have already said, Lysias' speeches are pervaded by a natural euphoniousness and grace. In this respect he excels all orators except Demosthenes. Well, this quality carries him on, like a south wind, as far as the proem and narration: but when he gets to the proof, it grows dim and faint: when he gets to the emotional part, it fails altogether. He has not much intensity or strength. But in Demosthenes there is a great deal of intensity and quite enough charm. So that his supremacy is due to an adequate and moderate share of the one quality and a superabundance of the other. Here is another hint for distinguishing Demosthenes' style, when it is confined to the limits of irreducible necessity. He does not, while divesting himself of strangeness, elaboration and all accessory ornament, at the same time sacrifice grandeur and intensity. These are qualities inseparable from his style, whether inborn or the result of practice. They admit however of a certain proportional rise and fall. All this is well known to my readers, and I need not give examples.

Thucydides' Influence on Demosthenes

DE THUCYDIDE § 53.

Demosthenes, alone among orators, imitated Thucydides in many particulars, as he imitated all writers who appeared to him to have achieved greatness and distinction. He acquired from him, and added to his own political speeches, merits which neither Antiphon, nor Lysias, nor Isocrates, the foremost orators of the day, possessed: I mean, swiftness, concentration, intensity, acrid pungency, and the force that arouses emotion.   On the other hand he neglected the recondite side of Thucydides' style, its strangeness and its poetical tinge, considering these qualities ill adapted to practical issues.   Nor did he approve of Thucydides' use of figures of speech, straying far from the natural sequence of ideas, nor of his solecisms.   He confined himself to the normal, while embellishing his diction with variety and diversity of expression, and absolutely never expressing any idea in a perfectly direct way.   His intricate sentences, which express much in a few words, sustain a lengthy grammatical connection, and make their point by an unexpected turn, Demosthenes emulated and introduced into his political and forensic speeches, using them more lavishly in public, than in private, suits.

The Greatness of Demosthenes

De Demosthene § 22.

When I read one of Isocrates' compositions, whether it be a forensic or a political speech, . . . I am filled with a high seriousness and my mind is completely calm, as though I were listening to the slow, solemn tones of the clarinet, or Dorian or enharmonic melodies.   But when I take up a work of Demosthenes, I am as one inspired, I am swept this way and that, one emotion follows another, incredulity, anxiety, fear, contempt, hatred, pity, sympathy, rage, envy, a succession of all the passions that can sway the human heart.   I think that at such times I am in exactly the same state as the initiates at the mysteries of the Mother or the Corybantes, or the like (whether it be smell, or sound, or the actual breath of the divinity that arouses in these persons such a galaxy of varied visions). Indeed I once reflected on the impression which the words of Demosthenes, uttered by himself, must have made on his contemporaries. When we, at such a distance of time, and unaffected ourselves by the issue, are so carried away and overcome, following wherever the words lead us, how must the Athenians and other Greeks of those days have been carried away by the man, when there was a real issue affecting them personally, and he was himself speaking his own words with that dignity which he possessed, and was expressing the emotions, nay, the transport of his own soul, beautifying every point and colouring it with the appropriate style of delivery, of which he was admittedly such a master. The speeches I have just quoted prove that of themselves. One cannot, even if one would, read them through at one's ease, as so much written matter. The very words teach one how to deliver them with the varying tones of irony, anger and reproach: terrifying, cajoling, admonishing, stimulating, producing in the utterance all the effects intended by the language. If the inspiration that after all these years still permeates the volumes has such power, such magic to draw men's hearts, how marvellous and overpowering must the effect of his speeches have been when actually delivered?

Dinarchus, the Eclectic Imitator

DE DINARCHO §§ 5–8.

Now that we have discovered the man's date, as accurately as possible, to help us in determining which of his speeches are genuine and which not, it is time to speak of his distinguishing characteristics. These are hard to define. He has no trait which is consistently found in him, or never found except in him, either in his private or in his public speeches. In different places he approximates to the styles of Lysias, of

Hyperides and of Demosthenes.   Many illustrations may be given of this.   The resemblance to Lysias is seen in the speech about Mnesicles, the speech against Lysicrates on behalf of Nicomachus, and many others.   Examples of the resemblance to Hyperides, who is more careful in his arrangement of material, and nobler in style than Lysias, may be found in more than thirty of Dinarchus' speeches, particularly in the demurrer in the case of Agathon.   But many more examples may be quoted of his resemblance to Demosthenes, whom he imitated above all: particularly in the speech against Polyeuctus.   The proem is similar to those of Demosthenes, and the resemblance goes right through the speech.

How then can one tell which speeches are really by Dinarchus ?   First of all, one must understand the characteristics of the other orators.   Then one must attribute to Dinarchus the speeches which resemble Lysias, pronounce, without troubling about title pages, that he is the author of others which some consider the work of Hyperides, and assert with all possible emphasis that those which approximate to the Demosthenic style are from the pen of this orator.   The other orators whom Dinarchus imitated may best be recognised by the homogeneity of their language.   Lysias, for example, in private and public speeches alike, preserves his own qualities consistently,[1] . . . and as regards style, lucidity of diction, and an arrangement of words, which is natural and smooth in appearance, but is more gratifying than any other prose.   Hyperides is inferior to Lysias in his choice of words, but superior to him in the sphere of subject matter.   He tells his story in different ways: sometimes in the natural order, sometimes beginning from the end.   He establishes his case not by suggestion alone,

[1] Words seem to be missing here, dealing with Lysias' treatment of subject-matter.

but also by full and formal demonstration. Demosthenes, who excelled not only these, but all other orators, imitated every model, and picked out the best wherever he found it. He reveals himself by the very language he talks, by the appropriateness which is found in every speech, and also by his arrangement of words, the close-knit texture of his figures, his disposition of matter, his emotional power, and, most of all, his force. Dinarchus on the other hand is not the same all through, nor is he the inventor of any-thing in particular by which one could recognise his style with certainty. It can only be recognised by its imitative character. For there is a great and obvious difference between imitator and originator. One may see that by comparing Isocrates with his school.

Let us suppose that we have certain speeches, attributed to Dinarchus, but greatly resembling Lysias. Whoever wishes to determine their authorship, must first consider the characteristics of Lysias. Then if he finds in these speeches the fine flower of excellence and charm, a tasteful choice of language, and no sign of lifelessness, he may boldly pro-nounce them to be by Lysias. But if he finds them inferior in grace, in power of persuasion, in sureness of expression, in grasp of reality, he may leave them among Dinarchus' works. The same is true of Hyperides. If the critic finds powerful language, simplicity of arrangement, appro-priateness of subject matter, and an absence of pretentiousness and bombast in the style, he may ascribe the works to Hyperides. These are the main features of his style. But if the work is deficient in these particular qualities, even if it is not at all bad in other respects, it had better be restored to Dinarchus. We may make the same supposition in the case of Demosthenes. If dignity of style, distinction of arrangement, living passion, pungency and intellectuality pervading every letter, inspiration, forcefulness are found throughout the work, do not hesitate to ascribe the work to Demosthenes. But if the complete manifestation of these qualities is lacking, or the homogeneity of the whole is imperfect, let the work remain among the writings of Dinarchus. Speaking broadly, we can discover two kinds of relationship between the ancient model and its modern imitation. There is the spontaneous imitation which is derived from long familiarity with an author and the repeated listening to his works. And there is the allied form of imitation based on text-book precepts. About the first, what can one say? And about the second, what remark is possible? This, that in all work which strikes out a new line there is a spontaneous grace and charm, whereas in derivative work, however perfect the imitation, there is something laboured and artificial. It is not only orators who distinguish between orators on this principle. The same test is used by painters, bronze-workers and sculptors for differentiating Apelles, Polyclitus, and Phidias from their respective schools.

Those who profess to imitate Plato, but are unable to acquire his antique flavour, his loftiness, his charm and beauty, but drag in tasteless and highflown expressions, are soon convicted in this way. And the same method will find out easily those authors who say they admire Thucydides, and have difficulty in acquiring his intensity, compactness, force and so on, while carefully picking out his abnormalities of construction and his obscurity. The same is true of the orators. Hyperides' followers miss his charm and his power, and become jejune, like the Rhodian school of rhetoricians, Artamenes, Aristocles, Philagrius, Molon and the rest. Those who model themselves on Isocrates become languid, frigid, diffuse, unrealistic. I mean such writers as Timaeus, Psaon, and Sosigenes. Those who selected Demosthenes, and aimed at his good points, have been praised for the excellence of their intentions, but they were unable to acquire the chief merits of his work. Dinarchus may be reckoned as the best of these. In his choice of language, he falls short of Demosthenes' forcefulness: in its arrangement, he lacks his variety in the use of figures, and his distinction. He shows inferior resource in debate by choosing arguments which are not novel and startling, but obvious and at any one's command. In the planning of a speech, he shows less skill in arranging and working out his points, in preparing his ground, in stealing a march on an opponent, and generally speaking in the technical apparatus of oratory. Above all, he has an inferior sense of proportion, seasonableness and appositeness. I mean, not that this is universally true, as though Dinarchus were successful in none of these particulars, but that it is broadly and predominantly true. This is in fact the reason why some people called him a " country Demosthenes," basing their opinion on his defective power of planning a speech. For a countryman differs in appearance from a townsman not in his bodily shape, but in the way in which he adorns and disposes of that shape.

Criticism of Plato's Style

SECOND LETTER TO POMPEIUS

The language of Plato, as I have said before, aspires to unite two several styles, the elevated and the plain. But it does not succeed equally in both. When it uses the plain, simple and unartificial mode of expression, it has an extraordinary charm and attraction. It is altogether pure and translucent, like the most transparent of streams, and it is correct and precise beyond that of any other writer who has adopted this mode of expression. It pursues familiar words and cultivates clearness, disdaining all extraneous ornament.   The gentle and imperceptible lapse of time invests it with a mellow tinge of antiquity; it still blooms in all its radiant vigour and beauty; a balmy breeze is wafted from it as though from meadows full of the most fragrant odours; and its clear utterance seems to show as little trace of loquacity as its elegance of display.   But when, as often happens, it rushes without restraint into unusual phraseology and embellished diction, it deteriorates greatly.   For it loses in charm, in purity of idiom, in lightness of touch. It obscures what is clear and makes it like unto darkness; it conveys the meaning in a prolix and circuitous way. When concise expression is needed, it lapses into tasteless periphrases, displaying a wealth of words.   Contemning the regular terms found in common use, it seeks after those which are newly coined, strange, or archaic.   It is in the sea of figurative diction that it labours most of all.   For it abounds in epithets and ill-timed metonymies.   It is harsh and loses sight of the point of contact in its metaphors.   It affects long and frequent allegories devoid of measure and fitness.   It revels, with juvenile and unseasonable pride, in the most wearisome poetical figures, particularly in those of Gorgias; and in " matters of this kind there is a good deal of the hierophant about him," as Demetrius of Phalerum has somewhere said as well as many others: for " not mine the word."

W. RHYS ROBERTS.

VI. LONGINUS

The Nature of the Sublime

You will remember, my dear Postumius Terentianus, that when we examined together the treatise of Caecilius on the Sublime, we found that it fell below the dignity of the whole subject, while it failed signally to grasp the essential points, and conveyed to its readers but little of that practical help which it should be a writer's principal aim to give. In every systematic treatise two things are required. The first is a statement of the subject; the other, which although second in order ranks higher in importance, is an indication of the methods by which we may attain our end. Now Caecilius seeks to show the nature of the sublime by countless instances as though our ignorance demanded it, but the consideration of the means whereby we may succeed in raising our own capacities to a certain pitch of elevation he has, strangely enough, omitted as unnecessary. However, it may be that the man ought not so much to be blamed for his shortcomings as praised for his happy thought and his enthusiasm. But since you have urged me, in my turn, to write a brief essay on the sublime for your special gratification, let us consider whether the views I have formed contain anything which will be of use to public men. You will yourself, friend, in accordance with your nature and with what is fitting, join me in appraising each detail with the utmost regard for truth; for he answered well who, when asked in what qualities we resemble the Gods, declared that we do so in benevolence and truth.[1]　As I am writing to you, good friend, who are well versed in literary studies, I feel almost absolved from the necessity of premising at any length that sublimity is a certain distinction and excellence in expression, and that it is from no other source than this that the greatest poets and writers have derived their eminence and gained an immortality of renown.　The effect of elevated language upon an audience is not persuasion but transport. At every time and in every way imposing speech, with the spell it throws over us, prevails over that which aims at persuasion and gratification.　Our persuasions we can usually control, but the influences of the sublime bring power and irresistible might to bear, and reign supreme over every hearer.　Similarly, we see skill in invention, and due order and arrangement of matter, emerging as the hard-won result not of one thing nor of two, but of the whole texture of the composition, whereas Sublimity flashing forth at the right moment scatters everything before it like a thunderbolt, and at once displays the power of the orator in all its plenitude.　But enough; for these reflections, and others like them, you can, I know well, dear Terentianus, yourself suggest from your own experience.

First of all we must raise the question whether there is such a thing as an art of the sublime or lofty.　Some hold that those are entirely in error who would bring such matters under the precepts of art.　A lofty tone, says one, is innate, and does not come by teaching; nature is the only art that can compass it.　Works of nature are, they think, made worse and altogether feebler when wizened by the rules of art.　But I maintain that this will be found to be otherwise if it be observed that, while nature as a rule is free and independent in matters of passion and elevation, yet is she wont not to act at random and utterly without system.　Further,

---

[1] From an unknown author.

nature is the original and vital underlying principle in all
cases, but system can define limits and fitting seasons, and
can also contribute the safest rules for use and practice.
Moreover, the expression of the sublime is more exposed
to danger when it goes its own way without the guidance
of knowledge,—when it is suffered to be unstable and un-
ballasted,—when it is left at the mercy of mere momentum
and ignorant audacity.   It is true that it often needs the
spur, but it is also true that it often needs the curb.[1]
Demosthenes expresses the view, with regard to human life
in general, that good fortune is the greatest of blessings,
while good counsel, which occupies the second place, is
hardly inferior in importance, since its absence contributes
inevitably to the ruin of the former.[2]   This we may apply
to diction, nature occupying the position of good fortune,
art that of good counsel.   Most important of all, we must
remember that the very fact that there are some elements of
expression which are in the hands of nature alone, can be
learnt from no other source than art.   If, I say, the critic
of those who desire to learn were to turn these matters over
in his mind he would no longer, it seems to me, regard
the discussion of the subject as superfluous or useless. . . .

> Quell they the oven's far-flung splendour-glow!
> Ha, let me but one hearth-abider mark—
> One flame wreath torrent-like I'll whirl on high;
> I'll burn the roof, to cinders shrivel it!—
> Nay, now my chant is not of noble strain.[3]

Such things are not tragic but pseudo-tragic—" flame-
wreaths," and " belching to the sky," and Boreas represented
as a " flute-player," and all the rest of it.   They are turbid
in expression and confused in imagery rather than the

---

[1] The exact reference is uncertain. The phrase is found more
than once in Greek literature.
[2] Demosth. *c. Aristocr.* 113.
[3] *Aeschylus.*—Translated by A. S. Way.

O

product of intensity, and each one of them, if examined in the light of day, sinks little by little from the terrible into the contemptible.   But since even in tragedy, which is in its very nature stately and prone to bombast, tasteless tumidity is unpardonable, still less, I presume, will it harmonise with the narration of fact.   And this is the ground on which the phrases of Gorgias of Leontini are ridiculed when he describes Xerxes as the " Zeus of the Persians " and vultures as " living tombs."   So is it with some of the expressions of Callisthenes which are not sublime but highflown, and still more with those of Cleitarchus, for the man is frivolous and blows, as Sophocles has it,

> Of pigmy hautboys: mouthpiece have they none.[1]

Other examples will be found in Amphicrates and Hegesias and Matris, for often when these writers seem to themselves to be inspired they are in no true frenzy but are simply trifling.

Altogether, tumidity seems particularly hard to avoid. The explanation is that all who aim at elevation are so anxious to escape the reproach of being weak and dry that they are carried, as by some strange law of nature, into the opposite extreme.   They put their trust in the maxim that " failure in a great attempt is at least a noble error." [2]   But evil are the swellings, both in the body and in diction, which are inflated and unreal, and threaten us with the reverse of our aim; for nothing, say they, is drier than a man who has the dropsy.   While tumidity desires to transcend the limits of the sublime, the defect which is termed puerility is the direct antithesis of elevation, for it is utterly low and mean and in real truth the most ignoble vice of style.   What, then, is this puerility ?   Clearly, a pedant's thoughts, which begin in learned trifling and end in frigidity.   Men slip into this kind of error because,

[1] *Sophocles.*—Translated by A. S. Way.
[2] From an unknown author.

while they aim at the uncommon and elaborate and most
of all at the attractive, they drift unawares into the tawdry
and affected. A third, and closely allied, kind of defect
in matters of passion is that which Theodorus used to call
parenthyrsus. By this is meant unseasonable and empty
passion, where no passion is required, or immoderate, where
moderation is needed. For men are often carried away,
as if by intoxication, into displays of emotion which are
not caused by the nature of the subject, but are purely
personal and wearisome. In consequence they seem to
hearers who are in no wise affected to act in an ungainly
way. And no wonder; for they are beside themselves,
while their hearers are not. But the question of the passions
we reserve for separate treatment.

W. Rhys Roberts.

The Test of Sublimity and its Sources

On the Sublime, cap. 7-9.

You must know, my dear friend, that it is with the sublime
as in the common life of man. In life nothing can be considered great which it is held great to despise. For instance,
riches, honours, distinctions, sovereignties, and all other
things which possess in abundance the external trappings of
the stage, will not seem, to a man of sense, to be supreme
blessings, since the very contempt of them is reckoned
good in no small degree, and in any case those who
could have them, but are high-souled enough to disdain
them, are more admired than those who have them. So
also in the case of sublimity in poems and prose writings,
we must consider whether some supposed examples have
not simply the appearance of elevation with many idle
accretions, so that when analysed they are found to be mere
vanity—objects which a noble nature will rather despise

than admire. For, as if instinctively, our soul is uplifted by the true sublime; it takes a proud flight, and is filled with joy and vaunting, as though it had itself produced what it has heard. When, therefore, a thing is heard repeatedly by a man of intelligence, who is well versed in literature, and its effect is not to dispose the soul to high thoughts, and it does not leave in the mind more food for reflexion than the words seem to convey, but falls, if examined carefully through and through, into disesteem, it cannot rank as true sublimity because it does not survive a first hearing. For that is really great which bears a repeated examination, and which it is difficult or rather impossible to withstand, and the memory of which is strong and hard to efface. In general, consider those examples of sublimity to be fine and genuine which please all and always. For when men of different pursuits, lives, ambitions, ages, languages, hold identical views on one and the same subject, then that verdict which results, so to speak, from a concert of discordant elements makes our faith in the object of admiration strong and unassailable.

There are, it may be said, five principal sources of elevated language. Beneath these five varieties there lies, as though it were a common foundation, the gift of discourse, which is indispensable. First and most important is the power of forming great conceptions, as we have elsewhere explained in our remarks on Xenophon. Secondly, there is vehement and inspired passion. These two components of the sublime are for the most part innate. Those which remain are partly the product of art. The due formation of figures deals with two sorts of figures, first those of thought and secondly those of expression. Next there is noble diction, which in turn comprises choice of words, and use of metaphors and elaboration of language. The fifth cause of elevation—one which is the fitting conclusion of all that have preceded it—is dignified and elevated composition. Come now, let us consider what is involved in each of these varieties, with this one remark by way of preface, that Caecilius has omitted some of the five divisions, for example, that of passion. Surely he is quite mistaken if he does so on the ground that these two, sublimity and passion, are a unity, and if it seems to him that they are by nature one and inseparable. For some passions are found which are far removed from sublimity and are of a low order, such as pity, grief and fear; and on the other hand there are many examples of the sublime which are independent of passion, such as the daring words of Homer with regard to the Aloadae, to take one out of numberless instances.

> Yea, Ossa in fury they strove to upheave on Olympus on high,
> With forest-clad Pelion above, that thence they might step to the sky.[1]

And so of the words which follow with still greater force :

> Ay, and the deed had they done.[2]

Among the orators, too, eulogies and ceremonial and occasional addresses contain on every side examples of dignity and elevation, but are for the most part void of passion. This is the reason why passionate speakers are the worst eulogists, and why, on the other hand, those who are apt in encomium are the least passionate. If, on the other hand, Caecilius thought that passion never contributes at all to sublimity, and if it was for this reason that he did not deem it worthy of mention, he is altogether deluded. I would affirm with confidence that there is no tone so lofty as that of genuine passion, in its right place, when it bursts out in a wild gust of mad enthusiasm and as it were fills the speakers' words with frenzy.

Now the first of the conditions mentioned, namely elevation

---

[1] *Odyss.* xi. 315, 316. [2] *Ibid.* 317.

of mind, holds the foremost rank among them all. We must, therefore, in this case also, although we have to do rather with an endowment than with an acquirement, nurture our souls (as far as that is possible) to thoughts sublime, and make them always pregnant, so to say, with noble inspiration. In what way, you may ask, is this to be done? Elsewhere I have written as follows:— "Sublimity is the echo of a great soul." Hence also a bare idea, by itself and without a spoken word, sometimes excites admiration just because of the greatness of soul implied. Thus the silence of Ajax in the Underworld is great and more sublime than words.[1] First, then, it is absolutely necessary to indicate the source of this elevation, namely, that the truly eloquent must be free from low and ignoble thoughts. For it is not possible that men with mean and servile ideas and aims prevailing throughout their lives should produce anything that is admirable and worthy of immortality. Great accents we expect to fall from the lips of those whose thoughts are deep and grave. Thus it is that stately speech comes naturally to the proudest spirits.

W. Rhys Roberts.

Importance of the Selection of Details illustrated from Sappho
On the Sublime, cap. 10.

Let us next consider whether we can point to anything further that contributes to sublimity of style. Now, there inhere in all things by nature certain constituents which are part and parcel of their substance. It must needs be, therefore, that we shall find one source of the sublime in the systematic selection of the most important elements, and the power of forming, by their mutual combination, what may be called one body. The former process attracts the

[1] *Odyss.* xi. 543.

hearer by the choice of the ideas, the latter by the aggrega-
tion of those chosen. For instance, Sappho everywhere
chooses the emotions that attend delirious passion from its
accompaniments in actual life. Wherein does she demon-
strate her supreme excellence? In the skill with which
she selects and binds together the most striking and vehement
circumstances of passion:—

> Peer of Gods he seemeth to me, the blissful
> Man who sits and gazes at thee before him,
> Close beside thee sits, and in silence hears thee
>   Silverly speaking,
>
> Laughing love's low laughter. Oh this, this only
> Stirs the troubled heart in my breast to tremble!
> For should I but see thee a little moment,
>   Straight is my voice hushed;
>
> Yea, my tongue is broken, and through and through me
> 'Neath the flesh impalpable fire runs tingling;
> Nothing see mine eyes, and a noise of roaring
>   Waves in my ear sounds!
>
> Sweat runs down in rivers, a tremor seizes
> All my limbs, and paler than grass in autumn,
> Caught by pains of menacing death, I falter,
>   Lost in the love-trance.

Are you not amazed how at one instant she summons,
as though they were all alien from herself and dispersed,
soul, body, ears, tongue, eyes, colour? Uniting contra-
dictions, she is, at one and the same time, hot and cold, in
her senses and out of her mind, for she is either terrified or
at the point of death. The effect desired is that not one
passion only should be seen in her, but a concourse of the
passions. All such things occur in the case of lovers, but
it is, as I said, the selection of the most striking of them and
their combination into a single whole that has produced the
singular excellence of the passage.

W. Rhys Roberts.

The Greatness of Plato : the Advantages of Imitation

ON THE SUBLIME, cap. 12–14.

With his vast riches Plato swells, like some sea, into a greatness which expands on every side.   Wherefore it is, I suppose, that the orator[1] in his utterance shows, as one who appeals more to the passions, all the glow of a fiery spirit.   Plato, on the other hand, firm-planted in his pride and magnificent stateliness, cannot indeed be accused of coldness, but he has not the same vehemence.   And it is in these same respects, my dear friend Terentianus, that it seems to me (supposing always that we Greeks are allowed to have an opinion upon the point) that Cicero differs from Demosthenes in elevated passages.   For the latter is characterised by sublimity which is for the most part rugged, Cicero by profusion.   Our orator, owing to the fact that in his vehemence,—aye, and in his speed, power and intensity,—he can as it were consume by fire and carry away all before him, may be compared to a thunderbolt or flash of lightning.   Cicero, on the other hand, it seems to me, after the manner of a wide-spread conflagration, rolls on with all-devouring flames, having within him an ample and abiding store of fire, distributed now at this point now at that, and fed by an unceasing succession.   This, however, you[2] will be better able to decide; but the great opportunity of Demosthenes' high-pitched elevation comes where intense utterance and vehement passion are in question, and in passages in which the audience is to be utterly enthralled.   The profusion of Cicero is in place where the hearer must be flooded with words, for it is appropriate to the treatment of commonplaces, and to perorations for the most part and digressions, and to all descriptive and declamatory passages, and to writings on

---

[1] Demosthenes.   [2] Sc. " you Romans."

history and natural science, and to many other departments of literature.

To return from my digression. Although Plato thus flows on with noiseless stream, he is none the less elevated. You know this because you have read the *Republic* and are familiar with his manner. " Those," says he, " who are destitute of wisdom and goodness and are ever present at carousals and the like are carried on the downward path, it seems, and wander thus throughout their life. They never look upwards to the truth, nor do they lift their heads, nor enjoy any pure and lasting pleasure, but like cattle they have their eyes ever cast downwards and bent upon the ground and upon their feeding-places, and they graze and grow fat and breed, and through their insatiate desire of these delights they kick and butt with horns and hoofs of iron and kill one another in their greed." [1]

This writer shows us, if only we were willing to pay him heed, that another way (beyond anything we have mentioned) leads to the sublime. And what, and what manner of way, may that be? It is the imitation and emulation of previous great poets and writers. And let this, my dear friend, be an aim to which we steadfastly apply ourselves. For many men are carried away by the spirit of others as if inspired, just as it is related of the Pythian priestess when she approaches the tripod, where there is a rift in the ground which (they say) exhales divine vapour. By heavenly power thus communicated she is impregnated, and straightway delivers oracles in virtue of the afflatus. Similarly from the great natures of the men of old there are borne in upon the souls of those who emulate them (as from sacred caves) what we may describe as *effluences*, so that even those who seem little likely to be possessed are thereby inspired and succumb to the spell of the others' greatness. Was

---

[1] Plato, *Rep.* ix. 586 A.

Herodotus alone a devoted imitator of Homer? No, Stesichorus even before his time, and Archilochus, and above all Plato, who from the great Homeric source drew to himself innumerable tributary streams. And perhaps, we should have found it necessary to prove this, point by point, had not Ammonius and his followers selected and recorded the particulars. This proceeding is not plagiarism; it is like taking an impression from beautiful forms or figures or other works of art. And it seems to me that there would not have been so fine a bloom of perfection on Plato's philosophical doctrines, and that he would not in many cases have found his way to poetical subject-matter and modes of expression, unless he had with all his heart and mind struggled with Homer for the primacy, entering the lists like a young champion matched against the man whom all admire, and showing perhaps too much love of contention and breaking a lance with him as it were, but deriving some profit from the contest none the less. For, as Hesiod says, " This strife is good for mortals." [1] And in truth that struggle for the crown of glory is noble and best deserves the victory in which even to be worsted by one's predecessors brings no discredit.

Accordingly, it is well that we ourselves also, when elaborating anything which requires lofty expression and elevated conception, should shape some idea in our minds as to how perchance Homer would have said this very thing, or how it would have been raised to the sublime by Plato or Demosthenes or by the historian Thucydides. For those personages, presenting themselves to us and inflaming our ardour and as it were illumining our path, will carry our minds in a mysterious way to the high standards of sublimity which are imaged within us. Still more effectual will it be to suggest this question to our thoughts, " What sort of

[1] Hes. *Works and Days* 24.

hearing would Homer, had he been present, or Demosthenes have given to this or that when said by me, or how would they have been affected by the other?" For the ordeal is indeed a severe one, if we presuppose such a tribunal and theatre for our own utterances, and imagine that we are undergoing a scrutiny of our writings before these great heroes, acting as judges and witnesses. A greater incentive still will be supplied if you add the question, "In what spirit will each succeeding age listen to me who have written thus?" But if one shrinks from the very thought of uttering aught that may transcend the term of his own life and time, the conceptions of his mind must necessarily be incomplete, blind, and as it were untimely born, since they are by no means brought to the perfection needed to ensure a futurity of fame.

W. RHYS ROBERTS.

Figures

ON THE SUBLIME, cap. 16–21.

Here, however, in due order comes the place assigned to Figures; for they, if handled in the proper manner, will contribute, as I have said, in no mean degree to sublimity. But since to treat thoroughly of them all at the present moment would be a great, or rather an endless task, we will now, with the object of proving our proposition, run over a few only of those which produce elevation of diction. Demosthenes is bringing forward a reasoned vindication of his public policy. What was the natural way of treating the subject? It was this, "You were not wrong, you who engaged in the struggle for the freedom of Greece. You have domestic warrant for it. For the warriors of Marathon did no wrong, nor they of Salamis, nor they of Plataea." [1]

---

[1] Cp. Dem. *de Cor.* 208.

When, however, as though suddenly inspired by heaven and as it were frenzied by the God of Prophecy, he utters his famous oath by the champions of Greece ("assuredly ye did no wrong; I swear it by those who at Marathon stood in the forefront of the danger "), in the public view by this one Figure of Adjuration, which I here term *Apostrophe*, he deifies his ancestors.   He brings home the thought that we ought to swear by those who have thus nobly died as we swear by Gods, and he fills the mind of the judges with the high spirit of those who there bore the brunt of the danger, and he has transformed the natural course of the argument into transcendent sublimity and passion and that secure belief which rests upon strange and prodigious oaths. He instils into the minds of his hearers the conviction— which acts as a medicine and an antidote—that they should, uplifted by these eulogies, feel no less proud of the fight against Philip than of the triumph at Marathon and Salamis. By all these means he carries his hearers clean away with him through the employment of a single figure.   It is said, indeed, that the germ of the oath is found in Eupolis:—

> For, by the fight I won at Marathon,
> No one shall vex my soul and rue it not.

But it is not sublime to swear by a person in any chance way; the sublimity depends upon the place and the manner and the circumstances and the motive.   Now in the passage of Eupolis there is nothing but the mere oath, addressed to the Athenians when still prosperous and in no need of comfort.   Furthermore, the poet in his oath has not made divinities of the men in order so to create in his hearers a worthy conception of their valour, but he has wandered away from those who stood in the forefront of the danger to an inanimate thing—the fight.   In Demosthenes the oath is framed for vanquished men, with the intention that Chaeroneia should no longer appear a failure to the

Athenians.   He gives them at one and the same time, as
I remarked, a demonstration that they have done no wrong,
an example, the sure evidence of oaths, a eulogy, an exhortation.   And since the orator was likely to be confronted
with the objection, " You are speaking of the *defeat* which
has attended your administration, and yet you swear by
victories," in what follows he consequently measures even
individual words, and chooses them unerringly, showing
that even in the revels of the imagination sobriety is required.
" Those," he says, " who stood in the forefront of the danger
at Marathon, and those who fought by sea at Salamis and
Artemisium, and those who stood in the ranks at Plataea."
Nowhere does he use the word " conquered," but at every
turn he has evaded any indication of the result, since it was
fortunate and the opposite of what happened at Chaeroneia.
So he at once rushes forward and carries his hearer off his
feet.   " All of whom," says he, " were accorded a public
burial by the state, Aeschines, and not *the successful only*."

I ought not, dear friend, to omit at this point an observation of my own, which shall be most concisely stated.   It is
that, by a sort of natural law, figures bring support to the
sublime, and on their part derive support in turn from it in
a wonderful degree.   Where and how, I will explain.
The cunning use of figures is peculiarly subject to suspicion,
and produces an impression of ambush, plot, fallacy.   This
is so when the plea is addressed to a judge with absolute
powers, and particularly to despots, kings, and leaders in
positions of superiority.   Such an one at once feels resent-
ment if, like a foolish boy, he is tricked by the paltry figures
of the oratorical craftsman.   Construing the fallacy into a
personal affront, sometimes he becomes quite wild with
rage, or if he controls his anger, steels himself utterly against
persuasive words.   Wherefore a figure is at its best when
the very fact that it is a figure escapes attention.

Accordingly, sublimity and passion form an antidote and a wonderful help against the mistrust which attends upon the use of figures. The art which craftily employs them lies hid and escapes all future suspicion, when once it has been associated with beauty and sublimity. A sufficient proof is the passage already adduced, " By the men of Marathon I swear." By what means has the orator here concealed the figure? Clearly, by the very excess of light. For just as all dim lights are extinguished in the blaze of the sun, so do the artifices of rhetoric fade from view when bathed in the pervading splendour of sublimity. Something like this happens also in the art of painting. For although light and shade, as depicted in colours, lie side by side upon the same surface, light nevertheless meets the vision first, and not only stands out, but also seems far nearer. So also with the manifestations of passion and the sublime in literature. They lie nearer to our minds through a sort of natural kinship and through their own radiance, and always strike our attention before the figures, whose art they throw into the shade and as it were keep in concealment.

But what are we next to say of questions and interrogations? Is it not precisely by the visualising qualities of these figures that Demosthenes strives to make his speeches far more effective and impressive? " Pray tell me,—tell me, you, sir,—do you wish to go about and inquire of one another, Is there any news? Why, what greater news could there be than this, that a Macedonian is subduing Greece? Is Philip dead? No; but he is ill. Dead or ill, what difference to you? Should anything happen to him, you will speedily create another Philip." [1] Again he says, " Let us sail against Macedonia. Where shall we find a landing-place? someone asks. The war itself will discover the weak places in Philip's position." [2] All this, if stated

[1] Dem. *Philipp.* i. 10.   [2] *Ibid.* 44.

plainly and directly, would have been altogether weaker. As it is, the excitement, and the rapid play of question and answer, and the plan of meeting his own objections as though they were urged by another, have by the help of the figure made the language used not only more elevated but also more convincing. For an exhibition of passion has a greater effect when it seems not to be studied by the speaker himself but to be inspired by the occasion; and questions asked and answered by oneself simulate a natural outburst of passion. For just as those who are interrogated by others experience a sudden excitement and answer the inquiry incisively and with the utmost candour, so the figure of question and answer leads the hearer to suppose that each deliberate thought is struck out and uttered on the spur of the moment, and so beguiles his reason. . . .

The words issue forth without connecting links and are poured out as it were, almost outstripping the speaker himself. " Locking their shields," says Xenophon, " they thrust fought slew fell." [1] And so with the words of Eurylochus:—

> We passed, as thou badst, Odysseus, midst twilight of oak-trees round.
> There amidst of the forest-glens a beautiful palace we found.[2]

For the lines detached from one another, but none the less hurried along, produce the impression of an agitation which interposes obstacles and at the same time adds impetuosity. This result Homer has produced by the omission of conjunctions.

A powerful effect usually attends the union of figures for a common object, when two or three mingle together as it were in partnership, and contribute a fund of strength, persuasiveness, beauty. Thus, in the speech against Meidias,

[1] Xen. *Hellen.* iv. 3, 19.   [2] *Odyss.* x. 251, 252.

examples will be found of *asyndeton*,[1] interwoven with
instances of *anaphora*[2] and *diatyposis*.[3]   " For the smiter
can do many things (some of which the sufferer cannot
even describe to another) by attitude, by look, by voice." [4]
Then, in order that the narrative may not, as it advances,
continue in the same groove (for continuance betokens
tranquillity, while passion—the transport and commotion of
the soul—sets order at defiance), straightway he hurries off
to other *Asyndeta* and *Repetitions*.   " By attitude, by look,
by voice, when he acts with insolence, when he acts like
an enemy, when he smites with his fists, when he smites
you like a slave."   By these words the orator produces
the same effect as the assailant—he strikes the mind of the
judges by the swift succession of blow on blow.   Starting
from this point again, as suddenly as a gust of wind, he makes
another attack.   " When smitten with blows of fists,"
he says, " when smitten upon the cheek.   These things
stir the blood, these drive men beyond themselves, when
unused to insult.   No one can, in describing them, convey
a notion of the indignity they imply."   So he maintains
throughout, though with continual variation, the essential
character of the *Repetitions* and *Asyndeta*.   In this way,
with him, order is disorderly, and on the other hand disorder
contains a certain element of order.

Come now, add, if you please, in these cases connecting
particles after the fashion of the followers of Isocrates.
" Furthermore, this fact too must not be overlooked that
the smiter may do many things, first by attitude, then by
look, then again by the mere voice."   You will feel, if you
transcribe the passage in this orderly fashion, that the rugged
impetuosity of passion, once you make it smooth and equable
by adding the copulatives, falls pointless and immediately

---

[1] Broken sentences.   [2] Repetition of words.
[3] Vivid description.   [4] Demosth. *in Mid.* 72.

loses all its fire. Just as the binding of the limbs of runners deprives them of their power of rapid motion, so also passion, when shackled by connecting links and other appendages, chafes at the restriction, for it loses the freedom of its advance and its rapid emission as though from an engine of war.

W. RHYS ROBERTS.

Periphrasis

ON THE SUBLIME cap. 28–29.

As to whether or no Periphrasis contributes to the sublime, no one, I think, will hesitate. For just as in music the so-called accompaniments bring out the charm of the melody, so also periphrasis often harmonises with the normal expression and adds greatly to its beauty, especially if it has a quality which is not inflated and dissonant but pleasantly tempered. Plato will furnish an instance in proof at the opening of his Funeral Oration. " In truth they have gained from us their rightful tribute, in the enjoyment of which they proceed along their destined path, escorted by their country publicly, and privately each by his kinsmen."[1] Death he calls " their destined path," and the tribute of accustomed rites he calls " being escorted publicly by their fatherland." Is it in a slight degree only that he has magnified the conception by the use of these words? Has he not rather, starting with unadorned diction, made it musical, and shed over it like a harmony the melodious rhythm which comes from periphrasis? And Xenophon says, " You regard toil as the guide to a joyous life. You have garnered in your souls the goodliest of all possessions and the fittest for warriors. For you rejoice more in praise than in all else."[2] In using, instead of " you are willing to toil," the words " you deem toil the guide to a joyous life,"

[1] Plato, *Menex.* 236 D.   [2] Xen. *Cyrop.* i. 5, 12.

P

and in expanding the rest of the sentence in like manner, he has annexed to his eulogy a lofty idea. And so with that inimitable phrase of Herodotus: " The goddess afflicted those Scythians who had pillaged the temple with an unsexing malady." [1]

A hazardous business, however, eminently hazardous is periphrasis, unless it be handled with discrimination; otherwise it speedily falls flat, with its odour of empty talk and its swelling amplitude. This is the reason why Plato (who is always strong in figurative language, and at times unseasonably so) is taunted because in his *Laws* he says that " neither gold nor silver treasure should be allowed to establish itself and abide in the city." [2] The critic says that, if he had been forbidding the possession of cattle, he would obviously have spoken of ovine and bovine treasure. But our parenthetical disquisition with regard to the use of figures as bearing upon the sublime has run to sufficient length, dear Terentianus; for all these things lend additional passion and animation to style, and passion is as intimately allied with sublimity as sketches of character with entertainment.

W. Rhys Roberts.

Genius more Important than Faultlessness

On the Sublime cap. 33–35.

Come, now, let us take some writer who is really immaculate and beyond reproach. Is it not worth while, on this very point, to raise the general question whether we ought to give the preference, in poems and prose writings, to grandeur with some attendant faults, or to success which is moderate but altogether sound and free from error ?

---

[1] Herod. i. 105.   [2] Plato, *Laws* 831 B.

Aye and further, whether a greater number of excellences, or excellences higher in quality, would in literature rightly bear away the palm? For these are inquiries appropriate to a treatise on the sublime, and they imperatively demand a settlement. For my part, I am well aware that lofty genius is far removed from flawlessness; for invariable accuracy incurs the risk of pettiness, and in the sublime, as in great fortunes, there must be something which is overlooked. It may be necessarily the case that low and average natures remain as a rule free from failing and in greater safety because they never run a risk or seek to scale the heights, while great endowments prove insecure because of their very greatness. In the second place, I am not ignorant that it naturally happens that the worse side of human character is always the more easily recognised, and that the memory of errors remains indelible, while that of excellences quickly dies away. I have myself noted not a few errors on the part of Homer and other writers of the greatest distinction, and the slips they have made afford me anything but pleasure. Still I do not term them wilful errors, but rather oversights of a random and casual kind, due to neglect and introduced with all the heedlessness of genius. Consequently I do not waver in my view that excellences higher in quality, even if not sustained throughout, should always on a comparison be voted the first place, because of their sheer elevation of spirit if for no other reason. Granted that Apollonius in his *Argonautica* shows himself a poet who does not trip, and that in his pastorals Theocritus is, except in a few externals, most happy, would you not, for all that, choose to be Homer rather than Apollonius? Again: does Eratosthenes in the *Erigone* (a little poem which is altogether free from flaw) show himself a greater poet than Archilochus with the rich and disorderly abundance which follows in his train and with that outburst of the divine spirit within him which it is difficult to bring under the rules of law ?   Once more: in lyric poetry would you prefer to be Bacchylides rather than Pindar ? And in tragedy to be Ion of Chios rather than—Sophocles ? It is true that Bacchylides and Ion are faultless and entirely elegant writers of the polished school, while Pindar and Sophocles, although at times they burn everything before them as it were in their swift career, are often extinguished unaccountably and fail most lamentably.   But would anyone in his senses regard all the compositions of Ion put together as an equivalent for the single play of the *Oedipus* ?

If successful writing were to be estimated by number of merits and not by the true criterion, thus judged Hyperides would be altogether superior to Demosthenes. For he has a greater variety of accents than Demosthenes and a greater number of excellences, and like the pentathlete he falls just below the top in every branch.   In all the contests he has to resign the first place to his rivals, while he maintains that place as against all ordinary persons.   Now Hyperides not only imitates all the strong points of Demosthenes with the exception of his composition, but he has embraced in a singular degree the excellences and graces of Lysias as well. For he talks with simplicity, where it is required, and does not adopt like Demosthenes one unvarying tone in all his utterances.   He possesses the gift of characterisation in a sweet and pleasant form and with a touch of piquancy. There are innumerable signs of wit in him—the most polished raillery, high-bred ease, supple skill in the contests of irony, jests not tasteless or rude after the well-known Attic manner but naturally suggested by the subject, clever ridicule, much comic power, biting satire with well-directed fun, and what may be termed an inimitable charm investing the whole.   He is excellently fitted by nature to excite pity; in narrating a fable he is facile, and with his pliant

spirit he is also most easily turned towards a digression (as
for instance in his rather poetical presentation of the story
of Leto), while he has treated his Funeral Oration in
the epideictic vein with probably unequalled success.
Demosthenes, on the other hand, is not an apt delineator
of character, he is not facile, he is anything but pliant or
epideictic, he is comparatively lacking in the entire list of
excellences just given. Where he forces himself to be
jocular and pleasant, he does not excite laughter but rather
becomes the subject of it, and when he wishes to approach
the region of charm, he is all the farther removed from it.
If he had attempted to write the short speech about Phryne or
about Athenogenes, he would have all the more commended
Hyperides to our regard. The good points of the latter,
however, many though they be, are wanting in elevation;
they are the staid utterances of a sober-hearted man and
leave the hearer unmoved, no one feeling terror when he
reads Hyperides. But Demosthenes draws—as from a
store—excellences allied to the highest sublimity and per-
fected to the utmost, the tone of lofty speech, living passions,
copiousness, readiness, speed (where it is legitimate), and
that power and vehemence of his which forbid approach.
Having, I say, absorbed bodily within himself these mighty
gifts which we may deem heaven-sent (for it would not
be right to term them *human*), he thus with the noble
qualities which are his own routs all comers even where
the qualities he does not possess are concerned, and over-
powers with thunder and with lightning the orators of
every age. One could sooner face with unflinching eyes
a descending thunderbolt than meet with steady gaze his
bursts of passion in their swift succession.

But in the case of Plato and Lysias there is, as I said, a
further point of difference. For not only in the degree of
his excellences, but also in their number, Lysias is much

inferior to Plato; and at the same time he surpasses him in his faults still more than he falls below him in his excellences.

What fact, then, was before the eyes of those superhuman writers who, aiming at everything that was highest in composition, contemned an all-pervading accuracy? This besides many other things, that Nature has appointed us men to be no base nor ignoble animals; but when she ushers us into life and into the vast universe as into some great assembly, to be as it were spectators of the mighty whole and the keenest aspirants for honour, forthwith she implants in our souls the unconquerable love of whatever is elevated and more divine than we. Wherefore not even the entire universe suffices for the thought and contemplation within the reach of the human mind, but our imaginations often pass beyond the bounds of space, and if we survey our life on every side and see how much more it everywhere abounds in what is striking, and great, and beautiful, we shall soon discern the purpose of our birth. This is why, by a sort of natural impulse, we admire not the small streams, useful and pellucid though they be, but the Nile, the Danube or the Rhine, and still more the Ocean. Nor do we view the tiny flame of our own kindling (guarded in lasting purity as its light ever is) with greater awe than the celestial fires though they are often shrouded in darkness; nor do we deem it a greater marvel than the craters of Etna, whose eruptions throw up stones from its depths and great masses of rock, and at times pour forth rivers of that pure and unmixed subterranean fire. In all such matters we may say that what is useful or necessary men regard as commonplace, while they reserve their admiration for that which is astounding.

Now as regards the manifestations of the sublime in literature, in which grandeur is never, as it sometimes is in nature, found apart from utility and advantage, it is fitting to observe at once that, though writers of this magnitude are far removed from faultlessness, they none the less all rise above what is mortal; that all other qualities prove their possessors to be men, but sublimity raises them near the majesty of God; and that while immunity from errors relieves from censure, it is grandeur that excites admiration. What need to add thereto that each of these supreme authors often redeems all his failures by a single sublime and happy touch, and (most important of all) that if one were to pick out and mass together the blunders of Homer, Demosthenes, Plato, and all the rest of the greatest writers, they would be found to be a very small part, nay an infinitesimal fraction, of the triumphs which those heroes achieve on every hand? This is the reason why the judgment of all posterity—a verdict which envy itself cannot convict of perversity—has brought and offered those meeds of victory which up to this day it guards intact and seems likely still to preserve,

> Long as earth's water shall flow, and her tall trees burgeon and bloom.[1]

In reply, however, to the writer who maintains that the faulty Colossus is not superior to the Spearman of Polycleitus, it is obvious to remark among many other things that in art the utmost exactitude is admired, grandeur in the works of nature; and that it is by nature that man is a being gifted with speech. In statues likeness to man is the quality required; in discourse we demand, as I said, that which transcends the human. Nevertheless — and the counsel about to be given reverts to the beginning of our memoir—since freedom from failings is for the most part the successful result of art, and excellence (though it may be unevenly sustained) the result of sublimity, the employment of art is in every way a fitting aid to

[1] From an unknown author.

nature; for it is the conjunction of the two which tends to ensure perfection.

Such are the decisions to which we have felt bound to come with regard to the questions proposed; but let every man cherish the view which pleases him best.

W. Rhys Roberts.

Composition

On the Sublime cap. 39.

The fifth of those elements contributing to the sublime which we mentioned, excellent friend, at the beginning, still remains to be dealt with, namely the arrangement of the words in a certain order. In regard to this, having already in two treatises sufficiently stated such results as our inquiry could compass, we will add, for the purpose of our present undertaking, only what is absolutely essential, namely the fact that harmonious arrangement is not only a natural source of persuasion and pleasure among men but also a wonderful instrument of lofty utterance and of passion. For does not the flute instil certain emotions into its hearers and as it were make them beside themselves and full of frenzy, and supplying a rhythmical movement constrain the listener to move rhythmically in accordance therewith and to conform himself to the melody, although he may be utterly ignorant of music? Yes, and the tones of the harp, although in themselves they signify nothing at all, often cast a wonderful spell, as you know, over an audience by means of the variations of sounds, by their pulsation against one another, and by their mingling in concert. And yet these are mere semblances and spurious copies of persuasion, not (as I have said) genuine activities of human nature. Are we not, then, to hold that composition (being a harmony of that language which

is implanted by nature in man and which appeals not to the
hearing only but to the soul itself), since it calls forth
manifold shapes of words, thoughts, deeds, beauty, melody, all
of them born at our birth and growing with our growth,
and since by means of the blending and variation of its own
tones it seeks to introduce into the minds of those who are
present the emotion which affects the speaker, and since it
always brings the audience to share in it and by the building
of phrase upon phrase raises a sublime and harmonious
structure: are we not, I say, to hold that harmony by these
selfsame means allures us and invariably disposes us to state-
liness and dignity and elevation and every emotion which
it contains within itself, gaining absolute mastery over our
minds ?   But it is folly to dispute concerning matters which
are generally admitted, since experience is proof sufficient.

                                    W. Rhys Roberts.

                            Rhythm

On the Sublime cap. 41.

   There is nothing in the sphere of the sublime that is
so lowering as broken and agitated movement of language,
such as is characteristic of pyrrhics and trochees and dichorees,
which fall altogether to the level of dance-music.   For all
over-rhythmical writing is at once felt to be affected and
finical and wholly lacking in passion owing to the monotony
of its superficial polish.   And the worst of it all is that,
just as petty lays draw their hearer away from the point
and compel his attention to themselves, so also over-
rhythmical style does not communicate the feeling of the
words but simply the feeling of the rhythm.   Sometimes,
indeed, the listeners knowing beforehand the due termina-
tions stamp their feet in time with the speaker, and as in
a dance give the right step in anticipation.   In like

manner those words are destitute of sublimity which lie too close together, and are cut up into short and tiny syllables, and are held together as if with wooden bolts by sheer inequality and ruggedness.

W. RHYS ROBERTS.

Cause of the Deterioration of Modern Literature

ON THE SUBLIME cap. 44.

It remains however (as I will not hesitate to add, in recognition of your love of knowledge) to clear up, my dear Terentianus, a question which a certain philosopher has recently mooted. " I wonder," he says, " as no doubt do many others, how it happens that in our time there are men who have the gift of persuasion to the utmost extent, and are well fitted for public life, and are keen and ready, and particularly rich in all the charms of language, yet there no longer arise really lofty and transcendent natures unless quite exceptionally. So great and world-wide a dearth of high utterance attends our age." " Can it be," he continued, " that we are to accept the trite explanation that democracy is the kind nursing-mother of genius, and that literary power may be said to share its rise and fall with democracy and democracy alone ? For freedom, it is said, has power to feed the imaginations of the lofty-minded and inspire hope, and where it prevails there spreads abroad the eagerness of mutual rivalry and the emulous pursuit of the foremost place. Moreover, owing to the prizes which are open to all under popular government, the mental excellences of the orator are continually exercised and sharpened, and as it were rubbed bright, and shine forth (as it is natural they should) with all the freedom which inspires the doings of the state. To-day," he went on, " we seem in our boyhood to learn the lessons of a righteous

servitude, being all but enswathed in its customs and obser-
vances, when our thoughts are yet young and tender,
and never tasting the fairest and most productive source of
eloquence (by which," he added, " I mean freedom), so
that we emerge in no other guise than that of sublime
flatterers." This is the reason, he maintained, why no
slave ever becomes an orator, although all other faculties
may belong to menials. In the slave there immediately
burst out signs of fettered liberty of speech, of the dungeon
as it were, of a man habituated to buffetings. "For
the day of slavery," as Homer has it, " takes away half our
manhood." [1] " Just as," he proceeded, " the cages (if what
I hear is true) in which are kept the Pygmies, commonly
called *nani*, not only hinder the growth of the creatures
confined within them, but actually attenuate them through
the bonds which beset their bodies, so one has aptly termed
all servitude (though it be most righteous) the cage of the
soul and a public prison-house." I answered him thus:
" It is easy, my good sir, and characteristic of human
nature, to find fault with the age in which one lives. But
consider whether it may not be true that it is not the world's
peace that ruins great natures, but far rather this war
illimitable which holds our desires in its grasp, aye, and further
still those passions which occupy as with troops our present
age and utterly harry and plunder it. For the love of
money (a disease from which we all now suffer sorely)
and the love of pleasure make us their thralls, or rather,
as one may say, drown us body and soul in the depths, the
love of riches being a malady which makes men petty, and
the love of pleasure one which makes them most ignoble.
On reflexion I cannot discover how it is possible for us,
if we value boundless wealth so highly, or (to speak more
truly) deify it, to avoid allowing the entrance into our

[1] *Odyss.* xvii. 322.

souls of the evils which are inseparable from it. For vast and unchecked wealth is accompanied, in close conjunction and step for step, as they say, by extravagance, and as soon as the former opens the gates of cities and houses, the latter immediately enters and abides. And when time has passed the pair build nests in the lives of men, as the wise say, and quickly give themselves to the rearing of offspring, and breed ostentation, and vanity, and luxury, no spurious progeny of theirs, but only too legitimate. If these children of wealth are permitted to come to maturity, straightway they beget in the soul inexorable masters—insolence, and lawlessness, and shamelessness. This must necessarily happen, and men will no longer lift up their eyes or have any further regard for fame, but the ruin of such lives will gradually reach its complete consummation and sublimities of soul fade and wither away and become contemptible, when men are lost in admiration of their own mortal parts and omit to exalt that which is immortal. For a man who has once accepted a bribe for a judicial decision cannot be an unbiassed and upright judge of what is just and honourable (since to the man who is venal his own interests must seem honourable and just), and the same is true where the entire life of each of us is ordered by bribes, and huntings after the death of others, and the laying of ambushes for legacies, while gain from any and every source we purchase —each one of us—at the price of life itself, being the slaves of pleasure. In an age which is ravaged by plagues so sore, is it possible for us to imagine that there is still left an unbiassed and incorruptible judge of works that are great and likely to reach posterity, or is it not rather the case that all are influenced in their decisions by the passion for gain? Nay, it is perhaps better for men like ourselves to be ruled than to be free, since our appetites, if let loose without restraint upon our neighbours like beasts from a

cage, would set the world on fire with deeds of evil.
Summing up, I maintained that among the banes of the
natures which our age produces must be reckoned that
half-heartedness in which the life of all of us with few excep-
tions is passed, for we do not labour or exert ourselves
except for the sake of praise and pleasure, never for those
solid benefits which are a worthy object of our own efforts
and the respect of others. But " 'tis best to leave
these riddles unresolved,"[1] and to proceed to what next
presents itself, namely the subject of the Passions, about
which I previously undertook to write in a separate treatise.
These form, as it seems to me, a material part of discourse
generally and of the Sublime itself.

W. RHYS ROBERTS.

[1] Eurip. *Electra* 379.

VII. DEMETRIUS

The Period

On Style §§ 10–18.

From the union of a number of these members and phrases are formed what are called " periods." Now the period is a collection of members or phrases, arranged dexterously to fit the thought to be expressed. For example: " Chiefly because I thought it was to the interest of the State that the law should be abrogated, but also for the sake of Chabrias' boy, I have agreed to plead, to the best of my ability, my clients' case." [1] This period, consisting of three members, has a certain bend and concentration at the end.

Aristotle defines the period thus: " A period is a form of expression which has a beginning and an end." [2] The definition is good and fitting. The very use of the word " period " implies that there has been a beginning at one point and will be an ending at another, and that we are hastening towards a definite goal as runners do when they leave the starting-place. For at the very beginning of their race the end of the course is manifest. Whence the name " period," the image being that of paths traversed in a circle. It may be said in general that a period is nothing more or less than a particular arrangement of words. If its circular form is destroyed and the arrangement changed, the subject-matter remains the same, but the period will have disappeared. This may be illustrated by some such alteration as the following in the period of Demosthenes already quoted: " I will support the complainants, men of

---

[1] Dem. *Lept. init.*   [2] Aristot. *Rhet.* iii. 9.

Athens. For Chabrias' son is dear to me, and much more so is the State, whose cause it is right for me to plead." No longer is there any period to be seen.

The origin of the period is as follows. There are two kinds of style. The first is termed the "compacted" style, as for example that which consists of periods. It is found in the discourses of Isocrates, Gorgias and Alcidamas, in which the periods succeed one another with no less regularity than the hexameters in the poetry of Homer. The second style bears the name of "disconnected," inasmuch as the members into which it is divided are not closely united. Hecataeus is an example; and so for the most part is Herodotus, and the older writers in general. Here is an instance: "Hecataeus of Miletus thus relates. I write these things as they seem to me to be true. For the tales told by the Greeks are, as it appears to me, many and absurd."[1] Here the members seem thrown upon one another in a hcap without the union or propping, and without the mutual support, which we find in periods.

The members in a periodic style may, in fact, be compared to the stones which support and hold together a vaulted roof. The members of the disconnected style resemble stones which are simply flung carelessly together and not built into a structure.

Consequently there is something polished and clean-cut in the older method of writing. It resembles ancient statues, the art of which was held to consist in their severe simplicity. The style of later writers is like the sculpture of Pheidias, since it already exhibits in some degree the union of elevation and finish.

My own view is that composition should neither, like that of Gorgias, consist wholly of a string of periods, nor be wholly disconnected like the ancient writings, but should

---

[1] Hecat. *Fragm.* 332.

rather combine the two methods. It will then be elaborate and simple at the same time, and possess the charm of both manners, being neither too untutored nor too artificial. Public speakers who employ accumulated periods are as giddy-pated as tipsy-men, and their hearers are sickened by the idle trick; sometimes, indeed, they audibly anticipate the conclusions of the orator's periods and declaim them in advance.

The shorter periods consist of two members, the longest of four. Anything beyond four would trespass beyond the symmetry of the period.

There are also periods composed of three members; and others consisting of a single member, which are called "simple" periods. Every member which possesses the requisite length and is rounded at the end forms a single-membered period. For example: "Herodotus of Halicarnassus sets forth in this History the result of his inquiries." [1] Again: "Clear expression floods with light the hearers' mind." [2] For the simple period these are the two essentials, the length of the member and its final rounding. If either of these conditions be wanting, there is no period.

In composite periods the last member should be longer than the rest, and should as it were contain and embrace them all. When the concluding member is long and stately, the period itself will be stately and impressive; otherwise it will be broken and as it were halting. The following is an instance of the period here recommended: "True grandeur consists not in saying grand things, but in doing things said, after saying them." [3]

W. Rhys Roberts.

[1] Herod. i. 1 init.
[2] From an unknown author.
[3] From an unknown author.

Metaphors

ON STYLE §§ 78–90.

In the first place, then, metaphors must be used; for they impart a special charm and grandeur to style. They should not be numerous, however; or we find ourselves writing dithyrambic poetry in place of prose. Nor yet should they be far-fetched, but natural and based on a true analogy. There is a resemblance, for instance, between a general, a pilot, and a charioteer; they are all in command. Accordingly it can correctly be said that a general pilots the State, and conversely that a pilot commands the ship.

Not all metaphors can, however, be used convertibly like the above. Homer could call the lower slope of Ida its " foot," but he could never have called a man's foot his " slope." [1]

When the metaphor seems daring, let it for greater security be converted into a simile. A simile is an expanded metaphor, as when, instead of saying " the orator Python was then rushing upon you in full flood," we add a word of comparison and say " was like a flood rushing upon you." [2] In this way we obtain a simile and a less risky expression, in the other way metaphor and greater danger. Plato's employment of metaphors rather than similes is, therefore, to be regarded as a risky feature of his style. Xenophon, on the other hand, prefers the simile.

In Aristotle's [3] judgment the so-called " active" metaphor is the best, wherein inanimate things are introduced in a state of activity as though they were animate, as in the passage describing the shaft:

Leapt on the foemen the arrow keen-whetted with eager wing, [4]

---

[1] Hom. *Il.* xx. 218. [2] Demosth. *de Cor.* 136.
[3] Aristot. *Rhet.* iii. 11. [4] Hom. *Il.* iv. 126.

Q

and in the words:

High-arched foam-creasted.[1]

All such expressions as "foam-crested" and "eager wing" suggest the activities of living creatures.

Some things are, however, expressed with greater clearness and precision by means of metaphors than by means of the precise terms themselves: e.g. "the battle shuddered."[2] No change of phrase could, by the employment of precise terms, give the meaning with greater truth and clearness. The poet has given the designation of "shuddering battle" to the clash of spears and the low and continuous sound which these make. In so doing he has seized upon the aforesaid "active" metaphor and has represented the battle as "shuddering" like a living thing.

We must, however, not lose sight of the fact that some metaphors conduce to triviality rather than to grandeur, even though the metaphor be employed in order to enhance the effect. An instance is the line:

And with thunder-trumpet pealing the boundless heaven rang round.[3]

The entire firmament when resounding ought not to have been likened to a resounding trumpet, unless on Homer's behalf the defence be advanced that high heaven resounded in the way in which the entire heaven would resound were it trumpeting.

Let us, therefore, consider a different kind of metaphor, one which leads to pettiness rather than to grandeur. Metaphors should be applied from the greater to the less, not the other way about. Xenophon, for example, says: "on the march a part of the line surged out."[4] He thus likens a swerving from the ranks to a surging of the sea,

---

[1] Hom. *Il.* xiii. 798.
[3] *Ibid.* xxi. 388.
[2] *Ibid.* 339.
[4] Xen. *Anab.* i.˟8, 18.

and applies this term to it. If, however, it were conversely to be said that the sea swerved from "line," the metaphor would possibly not be even appropriate; in any case it would be utterly trivial.

Some writers endeavour by the addition of epithets to safeguard metaphors which they consider risky. In this way Theognis applies to the bow the expression "lyre without chords" when describing an archer in the act of shooting.[1] It is a bold thing to apply the term "lyre" to a bow, but the metaphor is guarded by the qualification "without chords."

Usage, which is our teacher everywhere, is so particularly in regard to metaphors. Usage, in fact, clothes almost all conceptions in metaphor, and that with such a sure touch that we are hardly conscious of it. It calls a voice "silvery," a man "keen," a character "rugged," a speaker "long," and so on with metaphors in general, which are applied so tastefully that they pass for literal description.

My own rule for the use of metaphor in composition is the art—or nature—found in usage. Metaphors have in some cases been so well established by usage that we no longer require the literal expressions, but the metaphor has definitely usurped the place of the literal term. For instance, "the eye of the vine," and so forth.

The parts of the body, however, which are called "vertebra" ($\sigma\phi\acute{o}\nu\delta\nu\lambda o\varsigma$), "collar-bone" ($\kappa\lambda\epsilon\acute{\iota}\varsigma$), and "ribs" ($\kappa\tau\acute{\epsilon}\nu\epsilon\varsigma$), derive their names not from metaphor but from their resemblance to a spindle-whorl, a key, and a comb respectively.

When we turn a metaphor into a simile in the way above described, we must aim at conciseness. We must do no more than prefix some such word as "like," or we shall have a poetical image in place of a simile. Take, for example,

[1] Theog. trag., Nauck., p. 769.

the following passage of Xenophon : "like as a gallant hound charges a boar recklessly," and "like as a horse when untethered bounds proudly prancing over the plain." [1]   Such descriptions have the appearance not of simile but of poetical imagery.

These images should not be used in prose lightly nor without the greatest caution.—This concludes our sketch of the subject of metaphor.

W. RHYS ROBERTS.

Hyperbole

ON STYLE §§ 120–127.

There are, however, people who hold that we ought to use grand language of little things.   They regard this as a proof of surpassing power.   For my own part, I can forgive the rhetorician Polycrates who eulogised . . . like another Agamemnon with antitheses, metaphors, and every trick of eulogy.   He was jesting and not in earnest; the very inflation of his writing is but pleasantry.   I have no objection to jesting, as I say.   But fitness must be observed, whatever the subject; or in other words the style must be appropriate,—subdued for humble topics, lofty for high themes.

Xenophon obeys this rule when he says of the small and beautiful river Teleboas: "this was not a large river; beautiful it was, though."[2]   Through the conciseness of the construction, and through placing the "though" at the end of a sentence, he has almost brought before our very eyes a small river.   Another writer, on the contrary, when describing a river like the Teleboas, said that "it rushed from the hills of Laurium and disembogued into the sea," as though he were describing the cataracts of

---

[1] Xen. *Cyrop*. i. 4, 21.   [2] Xen. *Anab*. iv. 4, 3.

the Nile or the mouth of the Danube.[1]   All expressions of this kind are called " frigid."

Small things, however, may be magnified in another way, and that not an unbecoming but sometimes a necessary way, for instance when we wish to exalt a general who has succeeded in some small enterprises as though he had actually won great triumphs.   Or we may have to justify the ephor at Lacedaemon for scourging a man who played ball with a studied disregard of the custom of the country.   The offence at first strikes the ear as a trivial one.   Consequently we solemnly descant upon its gravity, pointing out that men who permit small malpractices open the way to more serious ones, and that we ought to punish for small transgressions rather than for great.   We shall, further, adduce the proverb " the thin end of the wedge," [2] showing how it bears upon this trifling offence; or we shall go so far as to maintain that no offence is trifling.

In this way, then, we may magnify a small success, though not at the cost of propriety.   As what is great can often be depreciated with advantage, so can what is lowly be exalted.

The most frigid of all figures is hyperbole, which is of three kinds, being expressed either in the form of likeness, as " a match for the winds in speed "; or of superiority, as " whiter than snow " ; [3] or of impossibility, as " with her head she has smitten the sky." [4]

Indeed, every hyperbole transcends the possible.   There could be nothing " whiter than snow," nor anything " a match for the winds in speed."   However, the particular hyperbole already mentioned is specially called " impossible." And so the very reason why every hyperbole seems, above all things, frigid, is that it suggests something impossible.

[1] From an unknown author.
[2] Cp. Hesiod, *Works and Days* 40.
[3] Hom. *Il.* x. 436.   [4] *Ibid.* iv. 443.

This is the chief reason also why the comic poets employ this figure. From the impossible they evolve the laughable, as when some one said hyperbolically of the voracity of the Persians that "they voided entire plains" and that "they carried bullocks in their jaws." [1]

Of the same character are the expressions "balder than the cloudless blue" and "lustier than a pumpkin." [2] Sappho's words "more golden than all gold" [3] are themselves hyperbolical and impossible, though from their very impossibility they derive charm, not frigidity. Indeed, one cannot sufficiently admire this in the divine Sappho, that by sheer genius she so handles a risky and seemingly unmanageable business as to invest it with charm.

W. RHYS ROBERTS.

The Epistolary Style

ON STYLE §§ 223–235.

We will next treat of the epistolary style, since it too should be plain. Artemon, the editor of Aristotle's *Letters*, says that a letter ought to be written in the same manner as a dialogue, a letter being regarded by him as one of the two sides of a dialogue.

There is perhaps some truth in what he says, but not the whole truth. The letter should be a little more studied than the dialogue, since the latter reproduces an extemporary utterance, while the former is committed to writing and is (in a way) sent as a gift.

Who (one may ask) would, in conversation with a friend, so express himself as does Aristotle when writing to Anti-

---

[1] From an unknown author.
[2] Sophron, *Fragmm.* 108, 34, Kaibel. *C. G. F.*
[3] Sappho, *Fragm.* 123, Bergk.

pater on the subject of the aged exile ? " If he is doomed
to wander to the uttermost parts of the earth, an exile
hopeless of return, it is clear that we cannot blame such men
should they wish to descend to Hades' hall." [1] A man who
conversed in that fashion would seem not to be talking but
to be making a display.

Frequent breaks in a sentence such as . . . . are
not appropriate in letters. Such breaks cause obscurity in
writing, and the gift of imitating conversation is a better
aid to debate than to writing. Consider the opening of
the *Euthydemus*: "Who was it, Socrates, with whom you
were conversing yesterday in the Lyceum ? Quite a large
crowd was surrounding your party." [2] And a little further
on Plato adds: " Nay, he seems to me to be some stranger,
the man with whom you were conversing. Who was he,
pray? " [3] All such imitative style better suits an actor;
it does not suit written letters.

The letter, like the dialogue, should abound in glimpses
of character. It may be said that everybody reveals his
own soul in his letters. In every other form of composition it is possible to discern the writer's character, but in
none so clearly as in the epistolary.

The length of a letter, no less than its style, must be
carefully regulated. Those that are too long, and further
are rather stilted in expression, are not in sober truth letters
but treatises with the heading " My dear So-and-So." This
is true of many of Plato's, and of that of Thucydides.

There should be a certain degree of freedom in the
structure of a letter. It is absurd to build up periods,
as if you were writing not a letter but a speech for the
law-courts. And such laboured letter-writing is not
merely absurd; it does not even obey the laws of friendship,

---

[1] Aristot. *Fragm.* 615 (ed. Berol.).
[2] Plato, *Euthyd.* 271 A.   [3] *Ibid.*

which demand that we should " call a spade a spade," as the proverb has it.

We must also remember that there are epistolary topics, as well as an epistolary style. Aristotle, who is thought to have been exceptionally successful in attaining the epistolary manner, says: " I have not written to you on this subject, since it was not fitted for a letter." [1]

If anybody should write of logical subtleties or questions of natural history in a letter, he writes indeed, but not a letter. A letter is designed to be the heart's good wishes in brief; it is the exposition of a simple subject in simple terms.

Its beauty consists in the expressions of friendship and the many proverbs which it contains. This last is the only philosophy admissible in it, the proverb being common property and popular in character. But the man who utters sententious maxims and exhortations seems to be no longer talking familiarly in a letter but to be speaking " ex cathedra."

Aristotle, however, sometimes uses certain forms of demonstration fitly in a letter. For instance, wishing to show that large towns and small have an equal claim to be well treated, he says: " The gods are as great in one as in the other; and since the Graces are gods, they will be placed by you in one no less than in the other." [2] The point he wishes to prove is fitted for a letter, and so is the proof itself.

Since occasionally we write to States or royal personages, such letters must be composed in a slightly heightened tone. It is right to have regard to the person to whom the letter is addressed. The heightening should not, however, be carried so far that we have a treatise in place of a letter,

---

[1] Aristot. *Fragm.* 620 (ed. Berol.).
[2] *Ibid.* 609 (ed. Berol.).

as is the case with those of Aristotle to Alexander and with that of Plato to Dion's friends.

In general it may be remarked that, from the point of view of expression, the letter should be a compound of two styles, viz. the graceful and the plain.—So much with regard to letter-writing and the plain style.

W. RHYS ROBERTS.

VIII. PLUTARCH

Aristophanes compared with Menander

<small>COMPARISON BETWEEN ARISTOPHANES AND MENANDER.[1]</small>

IN general and speaking broadly he[2] far prefers Menander.
He adds the following detailed criticism. There is an
element [he says] of low theatrical vulgarity in Aristophanes, which is quite absent in Menander. The educated novice is captivated by the former poet: but the
educated man will take no pleasure in him. I refer to
antitheses, jingles and plays on words. Menander uses
them sparingly, with appropriate reason, thinking them
worth careful handling. Aristophanes uses them freely,
unseasonably and tastelessly.

[*Plutarch proceeds to give instances from Aristophanes,
the effect of which cannot be reproduced in English.*]

The language of Aristophanes mixes up the tragic with
the comic, the stirring with the prosaic, the obscure with
the everyday, dignity and elevation with small-talk and
nauseating rubbish. And his style, which contains such
variety and inequality, does not even adapt itself to the
requirements of the occasion. I mean for instance that
solemnity befits a king, forcefulness an orator, naïveté a
woman, prosiness an ordinary individual, vulgarity a person
of low type. But Aristophanes assigns to his characters
any language that occurs to him, quite at haphazard. You
could never tell whether the speaker is son or father or
bumpkin or god or beldame or hero.

---

[1] This is an epitome of an essay by Plutarch on the subject. We
do not possess the original essay.
[2] Sc. Plutarch.

Menander's diction on the other hand is built up of stones so smoothed for the fitting, it is so tempered and harmonious, that, although it covers a wide range of emotion and character, and is adapted to persons of every type, it yet retains the appearance of unity, and holds fast to the uniformity of common normal language in every-day use. And if his subject ever does require a certain amount of noise and bombast, he takes the mute from his instrument and replaces it the next instant in the most convincing manner, and reduces his tone to the appropriate volume. Of all the famous craftsmen who ever lived, no cobbler ever made a shoe, no costumier a mask, no tailor a cloak which suited man or woman, old or young, master or slave indiscriminately. But Menander so blended his style, that it fitted all natures, all conditions and all ages. Yet he was young when he began, and died at the zenith of his powers as a writer and dramatist, at the very time when an author's style, according to Aristotle, makes its greatest advance. Any one who compares Menander's early works with those of his middle and later period, will realise what further progress he would probably have achieved, if he had lived.

Some dramatists write for the mob, others for the select few. It is difficult to name any one who had the qualities to suit both. Aristophanes at the same time fails to please the masses and cannot be endured by the cultivated. His poetry is like a *passée demi-mondaine*, who tries to pass for a married woman. The masses cannot abide his independent originality, the highbrows loathe his licentiousness and spitefulness. Menander has the happiest gift for making himself at home in the theatre, in the school, at the dinner table. Of all the glorious literature of Greece, his poetry is the most universally suitable for reading, for learning by heart and for acting. He has shown us what cleverness really means, irresistibly convincing in whatever he attempts, and enslaving the ear and mind wherever Greek is talked. Really, who but Menander makes it worth an educated man's while to go to the theatre ?   And when are theatres filled with literary connoisseurs at a comic performance ? At dinner, to what author do the pleasures of the table more justly give place and Dionysus yield precedence ?   When painters' eyes are worn out, they turn for relief to the tints of flowers and grass.   Just so the lovers of philosophy and literature find in Menander a rest from unrelieved and glaring colours, he receives them in a flowery shady meadow, full of pleasant breezes.

Menander's comedies abound in the salt of hallowed wit, which might have been drawn from the very seas which gave Aphrodite birth.   Aristophanic salt is stinging and rough to the taste, its pungency wounds and bites.   I do not know in what his much vaunted cleverness consists, whether in the words or in the characters.   Anyhow, he always represents the worst side of everything.   Rascality with him is not gentlemanly but ill-natured, rusticity not naïve but idiotic, comic things not amusing but ridiculous, love not sunny but licentious.   It really looks as though the fellow did not mean his poetry for any respectable person, but intended the obscenities for the licentious, and the virulent abuse for the jealous and spiteful.

The Duty of an Audience

How to Listen § 14.

Some people imagine that while the speaker has a task to perform, the listeners have none.   They expect him to come to his work after anxious thought and preparation. They for their part burst in on the scene without a moment's thought or consideration of their duties, exactly as if they had been asked to a dinner-party, and had only to enjoy

themselves while others toiled.   Why, one expects something from a guest at a party, if he is a gentleman, and
something much more from a member of an audience.   He
is a sharer in the discourse and the speaker's collaborator.
He has no business to criticise the speaker's errors mercilessly,
pulling him up word by word and point by point, while he
himself without any correction misbehaves himself and
commits many errors in taste as a listener.   Just as in a
game of ball the catcher must sway in rhythmical accord
with the thrower, so in discourse there is a sort of
rhythmical rapport between speaker and listener, if each
plays his proper part.

IX. DIO CHRYSOSTOM

*How the three great Athenian Dramatists treated the Story
of Philoctetes*

ORATION 52.

I GOT up about the first hour of the day, as I was not very
well and the morning air was as cool as autumn, though it
was midsummer.   I did my toilette and said my prayers,
and then I mounted my carriage and took a number of turns
in the ring at a most quiet and comfortable pace.   Then
I went for a walk, and rested a little.   After this I oiled
myself and washed, and after having something to eat,
took up some tragedies.   They were by pretty first-rate
authors, Aeschylus, Sophocles and Euripides, and were all
on the same subject, the theft or robbery of Philoctetes'
bow, whichever it should be called.   Anyhow, Philoctetes
was having his bow taken away by Odysseus and was
himself setting sail for Troy, mainly of his own free will,
but to a certain extent under the stress of necessity, after
being deprived of the weapon which was his means of susten-
ance in the island, his comfort in sickness, and his glory.
Well, I revelled in the spectacle and thought to myself that
if I had been at Athens in those days, I should not have
been able to see the three competing against one another.
Some people saw the youthful Sophocles competing with the
aged Aeschylus, or the aged Sophocles with the youthful
Euripides. But Euripides did not overlap Aeschylus. And,
besides that, it seldom or never happened that all used the

same subject in competition with one another. So I seemed
to be in clover, and to have a novel comfort in sickness.
I gave myself a splendid *mise en scène*, and tried to pay careful attention, as though I had been one of the judges at the
first performance. But on my oath I could not have pointed
to a single particular in which any of the three was deficient.
The loftiness and antique air of Aeschylus, and his daring
originality in thought and language, seemed appropriate to
tragedy and the old-world character of heroes. There was
no chicanery, or garrulity or smallness there. You know,
even his Odysseus, though he makes him shrewd and crafty
for the age in which he lived, is very far removed from
modern unscrupulousness. He would actually appear old-
fashioned when compared with modern affectations of
frankness and nobility. And further, he needed no trans-
formation at Athena's hands to prevent his being recognised
by Philoctetes, a device which Homer used and Euripides
after him. In fact a person who dislikes Aeschylus might
perhaps censure him for taking no trouble to make Philoctetes' failure to recognise Odysseus at all credible. But
Aeschylus may be defended against such a charge. The
mere lapse of ten years, it is true, was possibly insufficient to
account for Philoctetes' not recalling the other's features,
but Philoctetes' illness, his miserable plight and the fact
that he had lived on a desert island ever since, combined
to make the occurrence not impossible. Sickness and
misery have often produced this effect on a man's appearance.
Again, Aeschylus' chorus did not need to apologise, as
Euripides' chorus did. Both poets made the chorus consist
of Lemnians. But whereas Euripides at once made them
ask pardon for their former neglect, since they had never
come near Philoctetes or done anything for him all those
years, Aeschylus introduced his chorus without any ado,
which is far simpler and better suited to a tragedy:

though the other course is truer to real life.   If the poets
had been able to avoid all improbabilities in their tragedies,
it would perhaps have been reasonable not to admit this
improbability either.   As it is, they often make heralds
cover a journey of several days in a single day.   And
further, nothing in the world could make it possible that
none of the Lemnians should have visited him or troubled
about him at all.   I do not think he could have existed the
ten years without any help.   The probability is that he got
some help, but little and seldom, and that owing to the unpleasant nature of his malady no one chose to take him into
their house and nurse him.   Euripides at any rate makes
Actor, one of the Lemnians, visit Philoctetes as an old
acquaintance who has frequently met him before.   Again,
I think it is unreasonable to blame Aeschylus for making
Philoctetes narrate his desertion by the Greeks and the whole
of his story, as though they did not know it already.   Men
in misfortune often recount their troubles to those who
know them perfectly well already, and bore with their
perpetual narratives people who have no desire to listen.

Again, the deceit which Odysseus practised on Philoctetes
and the argument by which he won him over, are not only
more dignified, befitting a hero, not a Eurybatus or Pataecion,
but also, I think, more plausible.   What need was there for an
elaborate device and stratagem against a sick man, and a
bowman at that, whose arm of defence would have been
at once rendered useless, if anyone had come close up to
him ?   And then, too, the description of the disasters of
the Greeks, the death of Agamemnon, the execution of
Odysseus on a most dishonourable charge, and the general
corruption of the army, is not only useful for heartening
Philoctetes and making him more inclined to accept
Odysseus' company, but is in a way plausible as well, owing
to the long duration of the campaign, and the recent conse-

quences of Achilles' anger, when Hector almost set fire to the ships.

Euripides' intellectual power and his unremitting carefulness, in consequence of which he never passes over an improbability, and never deals with his subject simply, but always employs to the full the resources of expression, make him the exact obverse of Aeschylus. His genius is in the highest degree political and rhetorical, and capable of very greatly benefiting the reader. At the very start, he represents his Odysseus in the prologue as turning over political ideas in his mind, and in particular expressing anxiety that, while popularly considered wise and exceptionally intellectual, he may after all be the precise opposite. For when he might have lived comfortably without any worries, he is always voluntarily getting involved in troubles and dangers. He says the cause of this is the ambition of gifted and noble men, who in their desire for a good name and world-wide renown willingly encounter the greatest and severest trials. "For naught on earth's so proud as human kind." Then he explains in clear and precise language the subject of the play, and the reason for his coming to Lemnos. He says he was transformed by Athena, so that Philoctetes might not recognise him when he met him. (Here the dramatist follows Homer, who represented Odysseus as transformed by Athena when he met Eumaeus and Penelope and the rest.) He says an embassy is going to come from the Trojans to Philoctetes, to ask him to surrender himself and his arms to them at the price of the throne of Troy. Thus Euripides diversifies the action and discovers opportunities for speeches, possessing, as he obviously does, unparalleled resourcefulness in arguing both sides of a question. He makes Odysseus come on with Diomede, instead of alone. That is another Homeric touch. In general, as I have said, throughout the whole of the play, the action is managed in a most

R

skilful and convincing way, and there is quite marvellous power in the language. The dialogue is lucid, natural and realistic. The lyrics, besides being charming, have a strong moral appeal.

Sophocles seems to come midway between the two. He possesses neither the bold originality and simplicity of Aeschylus, nor the preciseness, shrewdness and political realism of Euripides. His poetry is noble and magnificent, full of tragic stateliness and splendour of language, combining great beauty with elevation and dignity. He manages his plot in the best and most convincing way of all. He makes Odysseus appear with Neoptolemus, it being fated that Troy should be captured by Neoptolemus and Philoctetes, armed with the bow of Herakles. He makes Odysseus keep out of the way himself and send Neoptolemus to Philoctetes, telling him what to do. He does not, like Aeschylus and Euripides, make his chorus consist of natives of the island, but of the sailors who sailed with Odysseus and Neoptolemus. The characters are marvellously dignified and noble. Odysseus is far gentler and franker than Euripides makes him. Neoptolemus is frank and chivalrous to the last degree. At first he refuses to overcome Philoctetes by craft and deceit, preferring to use open force. Then he is persuaded by Odysseus and does trick Philoctetes and gets possession of the bow: but when Philoctetes realises what has happened and is furious at the deceit, and asks for the bow back, he cannot endure it, but is ready to return the bow, though Odysseus appears and forbids him, and finally he does return it. After doing so, he tries to persuade Philoctetes to come with him voluntarily to Troy. And when Philoctetes will on no account yield or consent, but asks Neoptolemus to take him back to Greece, as he promised, he agrees and is ready to do so, till Herakles appears and persuades Philoctetes to

sail of his own will to Troy. The lyrics are not so full
of reflections, and do not make the same moral appeal, as
those in Euripides' play. But they are extraordinarily
beautiful and dignified. Aristophanes was not speaking at
random when he said:

> He used to lick the lips of Sophocles,
> Smeared o'er with sweetness like a honey-jar.

X. LUCIAN

How to become a Perfect Orator

THE ORATOR'S MANUAL §§ 15–21.

FIRST of all I will tell you what provisions you must bring from home for your journey, and how to replenish them, so that you may reach your destination as quickly as possible. Secondly, I will myself show you some things as you start on your way, and give you advice as to others. Thus, before the sun sets, I will make you into a supreme orator like myself, beyond any manner of question the beginning and middle and end of all who aspire to eloquence. Well, you must take as your staple ration stupidity, adding effrontery, recklessness and brazenness. Leave shame, decency, moderation, bashfulness at home. They are useless and will only hinder you. Take the loudest possible bellow, a devil-me-care voice and a walk like mine. That is all you really need, and is sometimes enough of itself. Your clothes must be white and embroidered, of Tarentine workmanship, made of transparent stuff. You must have Attic ladies' boots, the slit sort, or else Sicyonian shoes lined with white felt. You should have a numerous retinue, and always carry a book. So much for your own contribution: now mark how you are to supplement this *en route*. I am going to tell you the laws you must observe, if Rhetoric is to recognise you and take you to herself, not turn from you and "go-to-hell" you, as a profane spier out of her mysteries. First of all you must take particular care of your appearance and wear your clothes with an air.

218

Secondly, you must pick up somewhere fifteen to twenty
Attic words, learn them accurately by heart and have them
at the tip of your tongue, expressions like "divers," "there-
after," "say you so," "howsoe'er it be," "my sweet sir,"
and so on.   Lay them on thick like sauce in every speech.
Do not be disturbed if all the rest is quite different and
clashes incongruously.   Let but your purple tunic be gay
and lovely, even if your cloak is a coarse goatskin.   After
that collect some mysterious, rare words, used once or twice
by the ancients, and carefully discharge them at the company.
The masses will look up to you as a marvel of culture quite
above their heads, if you call washing "laving," a deposit
"earnest money," and dawn "the rim of the dark."   Sometimes you must yourself invent extraordinary new words,
and legislate that the man with a gift for expression must be
called "speechsome," the clever man "wise-heart," the
dancer a "hand-virtuoso."   If you perpetrate a solecism or a
grammatical blunder, your universal nostrum must be shamelessness.   You can produce in a moment the name of some
poet or prose writer who does not exist and never did.   He
was, you say, a genius, and a man of extremely polished
utterance, and he sanctioned your expression.   But don't
you ever read the old classics, that rubbishy Isocrates,
that dreary Demosthenes, that frigid Plato.   Read the
writings of the last generation, and those "exercises" they
talk of.   Then you can replenish your stock from them at
any time you wish, and draw from their store.   When
the moment for your speech arrives, and the company
proposes themes and subjects, say that all the difficult ones
are easy, and pour contempt on the timidity of their choice.
When they have made their selection, don't waste a moment,
but say whatever comes into your feckless head.   Don't
trouble to put things in their proper logical order, one, two,
three, but say what occurs to you first, even if the greave

does happen to be on the forehead, and the helmet on the shin. Only hurry, and leave no gaps, and never stop talking. If you are speaking about a bully or adulterer in Athens, describe what happens in India or at Ecbatana. Always mention Marathon and Cynaegeirus, these are indispensable. Always have people sailing through Mount Athos and walking over the Hellespont, and the sun shadowed by the Persian arrows and Xerxes running away, and Leonidas winning renown. And you must have the reading of Othryades' inscription, and plenty of Salamis and Artemisium and Plataea, and over all, as a sort of surface bloom, a succession of those little words "divers" and "methinks," even if they are quite superfluous. They are beautiful words, even when used at random. If you think it is time for a song, you may chant everything and make it a musical performance. And if ever you are at a loss for a subject for your song, you may appropriately fill up the gaps in the tune by enumerating the names of the jurymen. You must frequently exclaim "alas the day," and smite your thigh, and bellow and spit at the other man's speech and walk about waggling your buttocks. If the audience will not applaud you, take it amiss and abuse them. And if they get up for very shame and prepare to go out, tell them to sit down, and let the whole business be sheer tyranny. To make them admire your flow of words, you had better begin with the Trojan war or even the nuptials of Deucalion and Pyrrha, if you like, and so down to the present day. Few people have any discernment, and they will probably have the good nature to keep silence. If they do speak, it will look as if they did so out of jealousy. Most of the audience are struck dumb by your gait and your voice and your walk and your excursions up and down the platform, and your musical performance and your boots, and that "divers" of yours. Watching your sweat and your

laboured breathing, they are unable to resist the conclusion
that you are a monstrous fine exponent of the art of speaking.
And in particular, this rapidity covers a multitude of sins
and excites popular admiration.   So take care not to write
any notes or think your subject out, before you rise.   That
finds you out at once.   Your friends must keep stamping
hard and earn their dinner.   If they see that you are about
to break down, they must raise their hands and give you a
chance to find something to say in the intervals between
the applause.   In fact this is one of the things you must
be careful about, to have a chorus who will be loyal to you
and keep in tune with one another.

INDEX

223